Progressive Debate

BILAL QURESHI

ACTIVE 3

도서출판 청람

Preface

The Progressive Debate series consists of a string of articles on a variety of daily life issues in order to offer two-sided perspectives in each unit which can help learners connect their background knowledge to the topic. The most distinguished feature of this book series is the combination of warm up, pre reading and listening, and main comprehension exercises which develop learners' fluency and accuracy. These comprehension exercises allow students to fully grasp the topic in depth through the course of the whole series. The step by step progression of comprehension exercises engages learners to develop their knowledge for a more evocative conversation. These exercises lead students to develop their own unique perspectives about the topics and engage in meaningful conversation as a final goal.

Reading

A variety of daily life topics with lots of interesting and eye catching vocabulary words are one of the best features of this series of books. All articles are followed by a series of exercises that will certainly help learners improve their comprehension skills.

Discussion

Progressive Debate has been specifically designed to target discussion based classes. It further emphasizes students' need for all four components of language including speaking, reading, writing, and listening.

Writing

Through a systematic organization of comprehension exercises, learners are able to produce a well-organized paragraph in written form.

Step-by-step execution plan for Progressive Debate in Classroom

1. Brainstorm about the topic using questions given in the warm-up section.
2. Get ready for reading by completing pre-reading exercises. Match the target words to their synonyms and explore the meaning of useful expressions given in the contents.
3. Read or listen the content and find the main idea.
4. Find the answers to the comprehension questions in each article.
5. Fill in the blanks using the given words.
6. Complete the sentences by matching one from each section in exercise 3.
7. Fill in the blanks and complete the summary of the article. After filling in the blanks, summarize the important points of the whole article orally.
8. Find grammatical errors in sentences and correct them.
9. Engage your group mates in a discussion using the questions given in exercise 6. These questions will help learners develop their own opinions about the topics. Try to ask more follow up questions to explore your peers' opinions.
10. Read the question in exercise 7 carefully and brainstorm for ideas with your peers. Complete the writing task as a homework assignment.

Components

Student book & Online Audio Recordings for each Article.

Key Feature

The Progressive Debate Active series is a three level, speaking oriented series of books for intermediate proficiency level English learners.These books include a series of interesting and relevant daily life topics to help English learners enhance their communication skills by participating in classroom debate. The articles contain a wide range of vocabulary, useful expressions, and step-by-step comprehension exercises to help learners develop their opinions and express their ideas in more logical and fun ways. This book series proves to be the best solution for English learners' fluency development because of its unique organization of exercises that help to develop learners' ability and knowledge gradually.

Progressive Debate

Table of Content

Unit 01 Do University Students Need Long Vacations?

Warm Up Exercises

01 Answer these questions.

1. What is a semester?
2. Name at least 3 universities in your city.
3. Name at least three high schools in your area?

02 Put the words in right column.

School, Learning, Textbook, Games, Sports, Break time

Education	Recreation

Pre-Vocabulary Exercises

1 Match the words to their similar meaning.

1. academic	a. nevertheless
2. educator	b. related to education
3. refresher	c. to mirror
4. reflect	d. a reminder
5. regardless	e. teacher
6. resource	f. a chance
7. individual	g. supply
8. opportunity	h. a single person

2 Find the meaning of the following phrases.

1. Useful resource ______________________
2. Adult individual ______________________
3. Positive attitude ______________________
4. Extracurricular activities ______________________

Do University Students Need Long Vacations?

University education is becoming more and more popular among students in the modern age. With the rapid growth of science and technology, awareness of learning at the tertiary level is commonplace among youths. Korean university students' graduation rate tops OECD countries from 2007 to 2017. A balanced workload and vacation time offer ample relief to both students and educators to be prepared for challenging tertiary education. In contrast to the high and middle school vacation period, most universities offer rather longer summer and winter breaks. It is estimated that students get an average 9-week vacation during the summer and winter. However, some people criticize the long vacation university students have during the summer and winter. Do students really need long vacations after every 16-week academic semester?

People who think long vacations are helpful support their opinion with two main reasons. Firstly, students need some free time to peacefully reflect and implement their learning during one academic term. During the semester students are too busy taking all the courses they registered for. That requires them to do lots of homework for each subject, take many quizzes and tests, and do many projects. They are also expected to take active part in extracurricular activities during an academic semester. This keeps them extra busy and a bit stressed so that they do not generally get many chances to reflect upon what they learn. Long vacation times give them an opportunity to understand what has been taught and to implement those skills in their daily life. Secondly, long vacations help students to obtain real-life experience by adopting hobbies, traveling, or doing part-time jobs. These activities help them to become valuable members of society. Furthermore, Long vacations give instructors some time for self-development by taking some refresher courses, attending conferences, and preparing for the next semester.

On the other hand, critics of long vacations argue that it de-motivates students. Firstly, most students do not study at all during the whole period of two months that makes them lazy and dull. Most students end up regretting after the vacation that they have wasted a lot of time doing nothing during the vacation. A longer semester helps them to stay focused on their studies and their future goals. Secondly, long vacations are a waste of students' tuition. Most students pay high tuition for a semester that ends in 16 weeks. A longer semester may give them more chances to learn and to stay in touch with their peers and teachers. This may provide them feelings of satisfaction about their learning. In addition, short semesters keep the campuses empty for long periods of time during summer and winter breaks. That is a waste of such useful resources for students.

This is a long debate whether to have long vacations or not during summer and winter in universities. Both sides have equally important rationales about this issue. Being adults, it is important for the university students to be responsible of their own self-development and to stay focused on their future plans regardless of long or short vacation periods. Their positive attitudes and realistic approaches towards their learning help them throughout the year.

Main Exercises

1 Answer the questions.

Q1. How high is the university graduation rate in Korea compared to other countries?

Q2. What benefits do real-life experiences have on students?

Q3. How can staying in touch with peers and teachers benefit students?

Q4. Which is longer, high school vacations or university vacations?

Q5. How long is a university semester?

2 Fill up the blanks using the words below.

educators *academic* *refresher* *progress* *opportunity*

1. .... must not teach students about political beliefs.
2. It is important to have a .... every once in a while.
3. A vacation may be a great .... to experience new things.
4. .... may be hindered if people are too exhausted.
5. .... studies need significant funding.

3 Match the phrases to those given below.

1. Adult individuals must
2. Many students participate in extracurricular activities.
3. It is important to maintain a positive attitude.
4. Wood is an example of a useful resource.

a. Take full responsibility in their actions.

b. At all costs.

c. Which has many uses.

d. After school.

4 Summary

Fill the blanks up using the words given below and complete the summary.

modern, breaks, implement, refresher, lazy, semester, peers, responsible, focused

University education is becoming more popular in ______________ age. However, unlike middle and high schools, universities tend to have longer____________. Some view this as positive, because students need free time to peacefully reflect and _____________their learning during the break, and it also gives the instructor some time to self-develop by attending some _____________ courses or attending conferences. However, critics argue that a long break demoralizes students, making them ___________ and dull. Also, it is a waste of the students' tuition fee, and a longer ___________ plan may give students the chance to keep in touch with their ___________ and teachers. For university students, it is important to be ______________ for self-development while being ______________ on his or her studies.

5 Find the mistake in each sentence and correct the underlined words.

1. The average university semester is 16 months long.
2. Korean universities graduation rate are one of the highest in the world.
3. Some students take on part time jobs to earning extra money.
4. Vacations may making students lazy and dull.

6 Discussion Questions

Q1. How can we stay busy during vacations?

Q2. How can we obtain real life experiences?

Q3. What are some ways to reduce tuition fees?

Q4. Why is the rate of university graduation high in Korea?

Q5. How can teachers take professional development courses if the vacation is short?

7 Writing Time

Is it a good idea to have shorter vacation? What are the pros and cons of short vacation? State reasons and provide examples to support your opinion.

Unit 02 Should the Drinking Age Be Lowered?

Warm Up Exercises

01 Answer these questions.

1. What does it mean by drinking age?
2. What is drinking age in Korea?
3. Why is drinking age necessary?

02 Put the words in right column.

Colorless, Odorless, Drunken, Diversity, Wholesome, Risky

Alcohol	Water

Pre-Vocabulary Exercises

1 Match the words to their similar meaning.

1. Attitude	**a.** manner
2. Chronic	**b.** inquisitiveness
3. Harmonious	**c.** pride
4. Self-esteem	**d.** balanced
5. Beverage	**e.** grown
6. Curiosity	**f.** constant
7. Mature	**g.** drink

2 Find the meaning of the following phrases.

1. Feeling deprived ______________________________

2. Prime time ______________________________

3. Integrate into ______________________________

4. Generation gap ______________________________

Should the Drinking Age Be Lowered?

Do you know how old you must be to legally drink alcoholic beverages in Korea? The minimum legal age for drinking varies among countries from 16 to 21. However, the legal drinking age in Korea is 19. It is controversial as to whether to lower the drinking age in Korea or not. Some people think that imposing limits on teenagers' alcohol consumption may send a negative message that may hurt their self-esteem, whereas, experts believe that lowering the drinking age will cause more harm to the society than good. Will lowering the drinking age help Korean society?

Proponents of lowering the drinking age in Korea claim that it will help to improve the youth's personalities and attitudes towards society. Firstly, lowering the legal age of drinking will help teenagers to be more responsible and mature. A majority of teenagers, nonetheless, have tried alcoholic beverages at family events before reaching the age of 19. Therefore, lowering the legal drinking age will help them to integrate into the drinking culture more naturally at an earlier age instead of feeling deprived and to trying illegal ways to access alcohol in order to address their curiosity. Secondly, the legal minimum drinking age is usually set by older people with no input from the young. In some conservative countries, the older people who set the legal drinking age would want to increase the age even beyond 19, believing that they are helping the society. This may cause a generation gap and miscommunication between young adults and older people.

On the other hand, opponents of lowering drinking age in Korea argue that it could cause harm to society. Firstly, lowering the legal drinking age might be dangerous for teenagers' brain development. Alcohol consumption interferes with brain growth and causes chronic problems among young adults. Young people who are in the habit of drinking alcoholic beverages face various brain related problems including vulnerability to addiction, memory loss, depression, violence, and even suicide. Secondly, lowering the drinking age below 19 will pose many dangers for teenagers. In order to drink alcohol, teenagers may choose to go to bars and nightclubs which are extremely unsafe environments for them. The teenage years are a prime time in a human life to plan and shape their future. Indulging in alcoholic drinks can limit their personal development. This can also form the habit of relying on alcohol as a crutch for any good or bad situation.

In conclusion, both opponents and proponents have their opinions regarding whether to lower legal drinking age or not. Drinking alcohol seems like a personal choice that needs to be respected. However, it is important for citizens, especially young adults, to show responsibility and respect the laws and restrictions imposed by the government in order to retain a harmonious society.

Main Exercises

1 Answer the questions.

Q1. What is the minimum legal age for drinking in Korea?

Q2. Why is the generation gap a problem for setting drinking age?

Q3. How does alcohol deter teenagers' brain development?

Q4. Which problems are associated to drinking alcohol beverages?

Q5. Why do some people want to increase the age even beyond 19?

2 Fill up the blanks using the words below.

curiosity *beverage* *self-esteem* *attitude* *chronic*

1. The last failure didn't affect my ....
2. You need to change your .... Be polite to the elders.
3. The kid is full of ...., she touches everything she sees.
4. My father has a .... disease which is hardly cured.
5. I am so thirsty, I need a cool ....

3 Match the phrases to those given below.

1. The older people would want to increase the age even beyond 19.
2. Some young people are in the habit of drinking alcoholic beverages.
3. A majority of teenagers, nonetheless, have tried alcoholic beverages at family events before reaching the age of 19.
4. The legal minimum drinking age is usually set by older people.

a. They may face various brain related problems.

b. Lowering the legal drinking age will help them to integrate into the drinking culture more naturally.

c. They believe that they are helping the society.

d. It is without input from the young.

4 Summary

Fill the blanks up using the words given below and complete the summary.

nightclubs, laws, benefit, brain, consumption, mature, generation

Some people think that imposing limits on teenagers' alcohol ________________ may send a negative message that may hurt their self-esteem. At the same time, experts believe that lowering the drinking age will cause more harm to the society than ________________. Proponents of lowering the drinking age in Korea believe it will help teenagers to be more responsible and ________________. Moreover, the reality that the older people set the legal drinking age may cause a ________________gap and miscommunication between young adults and older people. On the other hand, opponents of lowering drinking age in Korea claim that be dangerous for teenagers' ________________development since alcohol damages brain. Furthermore, teenagers may go to bars and ________________which are extremely unsafe. In conclusion, it is important for the citizens to show responsibility and respect the ________________and restrictions imposed by the government in order to retain a harmonious society.

5 Find the mistake in each sentence and correct it by reshaping the underlined words.

1. There is a controversial issue if lower the drinking age in Korea or not.
2. It will help for improve their personalities.
3. Lowering legal age of drinking will help teenagers to be more responsibility.
4. It will help them to integrate from the drinking culture.
5. Lowering the legal drinking age might be dangerous in teenagers.

6 Discussion Questions

1. Is 19 a proper drinking age? Why or why not?
2. Why shouldn't teenagers drink alcohol?
3. Which country has the lowest drinking age?
4. Which country has the highest drinking age?
5. What is the advantage of drinking alcoholic beverages?

7 Writing Time

Should Korea lower or raise the drinking age. Provide reasons and examples to support your opinion.

Unit 03 Can Money Buy Happiness?

Warm Up Exercises

01 **Answer these questions.**

1. What is happiness?
2. Name 3 things that make you feel happy?
3. Can money buy happiness?

02 **Put the words in right column.**

Sorrowful, Satisfied, Gloomy, Glad, Depressed, Frustrated, Pleased, Proud

Happiness	Sadness

Pre-Vocabulary Exercises

1 Match the words to their similar meaning.

1. Vice	**a.** approximately
2. Income	**b.** crime
3. Roughly	**c.** method
4. Factor	**d.** earnings
5. Formula	**e.** oppose
6. Deny	**f.** dissatisfaction
7. Frustration	**g.** element

2 Find the meaning of the following phrases.

1. Happiness level ______________________________

2. Contribute to ______________________________

3. Ultimate goal ______________________________

4. End up ______________________________

Can Money Buy Happiness?

We are all quite familiar with the phrase “money can’t buy happiness”. There is endless discussion about how much money is needed to make people happy. Studies show that for most people, happiness levels increase with the income up to roughly $50,000 per year. After that level, the relation between income and happiness is negligible. The race to earn more and more money to get happiness has existed since the beginning of currency. Many people believe money is the most important factor in their life that brings happiness, whereas; others insist that the desire to earn more and more money is only a formula to be stressed which denies these same people the happiness they are searching for in money.

Proponents of earning more and more money argue that it is the most important contributor to our happiness. Firstly, for many people, money is the ultimate goal of a successful life. They claim that the importance of money is easy to see by looking at someone who doesn’t have any. A higher income can give people access to beautiful homes, safer neighborhoods, better food to enjoy, good health, and more free time to spend with family or friends. Secondly, money provides people with chances to buy what they need, travel to different parts of the world, and enjoy hobbies that they like. Without money, people may feel a serious depression that may even lead them to commit crimes in order to fulfil their desires. In addition, money provides chances to learn new things like taking piano or violin lessons, learning skydiving, etc. For most people, learning new skills gives excitement and further, happiness.

On the contrary, opponents of money as an important source of happiness argue that those who believe in money can provide them with happiness end up in frustration. Firstly, when the income reaches a certain level meeting a human's basic needs including food, health care, safety, and housing, it loses its attraction. The excitement of earning money fades away with long working hours, stressful jobs, and improper working environments. Secondly, people who habitually buy new things eventually lose interest in those same things. Their desire drives them to buy more expensive items. In addition, excessive money may provide people opportunities to get addicted to drugs, alcohol, or other vices that may eventually lead them to depression or even suicidal tendencies.

In conclusion, the arguments against and in favor of gaining happiness through money have similar importance. While wealth doesn't necessarily bring happiness, overdue bills, massive debt, and unpaid tuition fees will definitely make people unhappy. It sounds realistic that having the money to meet the basic needs is important; however, to completely rely on money in order to get happiness can cause various social or moral problems. The most important thing to lead a happy life is to maintain a balance between earning and spending, to reduce reliance on money as a source of happiness, and to control unnecessary desires.

Main Exercises

1 Answer the questions.

Q1. To what extent can money make people happy?

Q2. Who wants to buy more expensive items?

Q3. Why do people who habitually buy new things eventually lose interest?

Q4. What can cause people to get addicted to drugs, alcohol, or other vices?

Q5. Why would poor people commit crimes?

2 Fill up the blanks using the words below.

denied *income* *frustration* *factor* *roughly*

1. Most CEOs have a high ....
2. 100 hours is .... 5 days.
3. Global warming is the main .... of this hot weather.
4. He .... that he betrayed me.
5. The failure leads to ....

3 Match the phrases to those given below.

1. Even if wealth dosen't necessarily bring happiness.
2. The race to earn more and more money to get happiness has existed.
3. Some people claim that the importance of money is easy to see.
4. The excitement of earning money fades away.

a. By looking at someone who doesn't have any.
b. Massive debt will definitely make people unhappy.
c. Since the beginning of currency.
d. When working hours are long and the job is stressful.

4 Summary

Fill the blanks up using the words given below and complete the summary.

source, addicted, chances, brings, attraction, more and more, neighborhoods

Many people believe money is the most important factor in their life that ________________ happiness. However, other insists that the desire to earn ________________money is only a formula to be stressed. Proponents of earning more and more money insist money is the ultimate goal of a successful life including beautiful homes, safer ________________, better food, good health, and more free time. Moreover, money provides people with ________________ to buy and enjoy what they need. On the other hand, opponents of money as an important ________________ of happiness argue that when the income touches a certain level, it loses its ________________ . In addition, excessive money may provide people opportunities to get ________________ to vices. In conclusion, the most important thing to lead a happy life is to maintain a balance between earning and spending, to reduce reliance on money as a source of happiness, and to control unnecessary desires.

5 Find the mistake in each sentence and correct it by reshaping the underlined words.

1. There is endless discussion about how many money can make people happy.
2. The relation between income and happiness are very little.
3. The race to earn more and more has existing since the beginning of currency.
4. Money can provide them with happiness end up for frustration.
5. The excitement of earn money fades away with long working hours.

6 Discussion Questions

1. What makes you feel happy?
2. Does money make you happy? Why or why not?
3. How much money can make you happy?
4. Why are rich people more likely to get addicted to drugs and alcohol?
5. What do you want to do if you had 1,000,000,000won?

7 Writing Time

What is your goal of life? Is it earning money or something else? Provide reasons and examples to support your opinion.

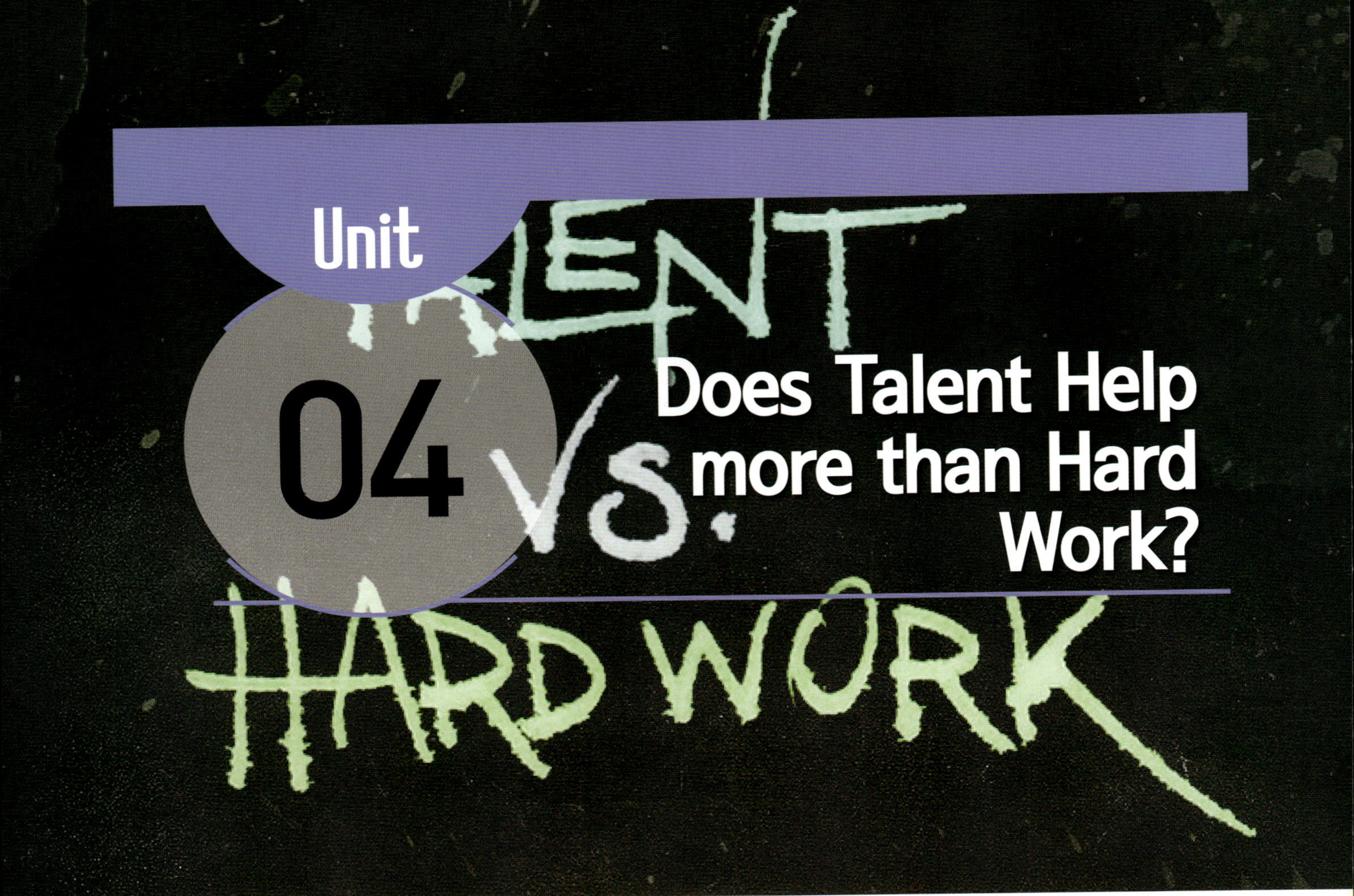

Unit 04 Does Talent Help more than Hard Work?

Warm Up Exercises

01 **Answer these questions.**

1. What does it mean by 'talent'?
2. Which talent do you have?
3. Which talent do you want to have?

02 **Put the words in right column.**

Inborn, Inherited, Effort, Easy-to-get, Blessed, Labor, Strive

Talent	Hard work

Pre-Vocabulary Exercises

1 Match the words to their similar meaning.

1. Struggle	**a.** individual
2. Entity	**b.** passionate
3. Opposite	**c.** strive
4. Enthusiastic	**d.** approval
5. Obstacle	**e.** contrary
6. Wit	**f.** barrier
7. Blessing	**g.** cleverness

2 Find the meaning of the following phrases.

1. Present-mindedness ______________________

2. Over-confident ______________________

3. Of no use ______________________

4. By definition ______________________

Does Talent Help more than Hard Work?

Among the many ongoing struggles between opposite entities in human life including men and women, tall and short, and black and white, one of the most durable battles is the debate about the roles of talent and hard work. This seems like a chicken and an egg puzzle; which comes first? By definition both are totally opposite terms where talent is someone's inborn quality that is inherited and allows a person to achieve goals with less effort in shorter time while hard work is someone's constant effort to achieve a chosen goal. In general, only a determined and enthusiastic person does his best to accomplish a goal without caring about the troubles, obstacles, and hurdles. Some people think that talent contributes more to an individual's success, while, others consider hard work an important key to success.

Advocates of the role of talent believe that it enables people to succeed in a comparatively short amount of time. Firstly, intelligence and present-mindedness play an important role in their rapid progress. They have quick wits and are generally swift in making their decisions. This ability easily reveals their aptitude to the people around them which further promotes their development. Secondly, talent helps people solve problems easily. Their strong instincts play a major role in handling various challenging issues. This gives them a chance to play a leading role in their communities and they easily gain people's trust and support in order to make important decisions.

Proponents of hard work argue that talent is nothing without hard work. Firstly, lots of people value hard work more than talent. It is quite difficult to deny the importance of hard work. All famous people who were talented were only able to bring that talent to bear through hard work. Mozart, Einstein, and all other successful people are called geniuses because of their persistent effort. Secondly, having the feeling of being talented can cause some people to become lazy. They may consider that their talent will help them to get their job done in a shorter time, which may not always prove true. Many students, who are told that they are smart, become overconfident and pay less attention to their studies that could cause timely embarrassment. Nevertheless, inborn talent is of no use if persistent work and effort are not invested to achieve a goal. Similarly, a person who has not inherited some special gifts, but has set a goal and does his best to achieve it has many chances to be successful.

In conclusion, both hard work and talent are important for attaining success; however, the answer to the question which is more likely to contribute to success in life is still uncertain. The only obvious assumption is that when a talented person works persistently, they have more chances to get success and joy. A person may have a talent, but they may never be aware of it, so realizing child's talent is a great blessing. Furthermore, these talents can be developed more to have greater positive effects on people's lives. Talent will be of no use and loses its value if it is not recognized and developed through hard work.

Main Exercises

1 Answer the questions.

Q1. What kind of people are swift in making their decisions?

Q2. What helps people solve problems easily?

Q3. What are Mozart and Einstein called?

Q4. Which bad impact does talent have on some people?

Q5. What does inborn talent need?

2 Fill up the blanks using the words below.

enthusiastic *opposite* *obstacle* *blessing* *struggle*

1. They .... for survival.
2. My home is located .... to the police station.
3. The audience in the concert was ....
4. We have to remove the .... on the road for the safety.
5. May the .... of God be upon you.

3 Match the phrases to those given below.

1. Talented people's strong instincts play a major role in handling challenging issues.
2. Lots of people value hard work more than talent.
3. Mozart, Einstein, and all other successful people are called genius
4. They may consider that their talent will help them to get their job done in a short time.

a. It is quite difficult to deny the importance of hard work.

b. It could prove wrong later.

c. This gives them a chance to play a leading role in their communities

d. Because of their persistent efforts.

4 Summary

Fill the blanks up using the words given below and complete the summary.

contributes, role, recognized, deny, key, feeling, solve

There has been the debate about the roles of talent and hard work for a long time. Some people think that talent ______________ more to an individual's success, while, others consider hard work an important ______________ to success. Advocates of the role of talent believe that talent plays an important ______________ in their rapid progress. Secondly, they also think talent helps people ______________ problems easily. On the other hand, Proponents of hard work argue that lots of people value hard work more than talent and it is difficult to ______________ the importance of hard work. Furthermore, having the ______________ of being talented can cause some people to become lazy. In conclusion, it is obvious that talent will be of no use and loses its value if it is not ______________ and developed through hard work.

5 Find the mistake in each sentence and correct it by reshaping the underlined words.

1. This seems like a chicken and an egg puzzle; which come first?
2. Some people consider hard work an important key for success.
3. Successful people are calling genius because of their persistent efforts.
4. Inborn talent is by nouse if persistent work and effort are not invested
5. Both is totally opposite terms.

6 Discussion Questions

1. What is the most common problem of talented people?
2. Do you know any genius who did achieve success in their field?
3. What kind of person are you? Talented or hard worker?
4. What kind of talents do you have?
5. What kind of talents do you lack?

7 Writing Time

Which is more important, talent or hard work? Provide reasons and examples to support your opinion.

Unit 05 Can Mobile Police Stations Control Crimes?

Warm Up Exercises

01 **Answer these questions.**

1. What is a mobile police station?
2. Have you ever visited a police station?
3. Which services do police stations offer?

02 **Put the words in right column.**

Crime, Taser gun, Textbook, Handcuffs, Academics, Uniform, Patrol car, Blackboard

Police officer	Teacher

Pre-Vocabulary Exercises

1 Match the words to their similar meaning.

1. Unimaginable	**a.** defenseless
2. Civilization	**b.** substitute
3. Chaos	**c.** inconceivable
4. Replace	**d.** judgment
5. Trial	**e.** society
6. Vulnerable	**f.** area
7. Precinct	**g.** disorder

2 Find the meaning of the following phrases.

1. Carry weight ______________________________

2. Investigative equipment ______________________________

3. Sense of security ______________________________

4. Handling crime ______________________________

Can Mobile Police Stations Control Crimes?

Have you ever imagined living in a world where there is no one to turn to when you feel your life is in danger? Life would be unimaginable, and civilization would be complete chaos. The police force is one of the most important institutions in every society that keeps the citizens safe. Police stations are control centers from where the whole law and order system is controlled. However, in this age of science and technology, many people think that traditional police stations should be replaced by mobile police stations. They think that large police station buildings are of no importance these days and are just a waste of resources. Do you think we should replace police stations with mobile police stations?

Proponents of police stations argue that they are one of the most reliable and easy to access resources for the public. Firstly, most police stations are equipped with the latest investigative equipment that is required for maintaining peace in community. Also, most police stations are equipped with holding facilities to keep criminals before trial. Secondly, a police station is a secure building that gives people of that community a sense of security. Not having a police station around may give the community a sense of uncertainty. In addition, police officers may feel vulnerable if they have no real station and that they need to be in mobile police stations all the time.

Opponents of police stations argue that these buildings are such a waste of resources and are not very efficient at handling crime. Firstly, they think that governments spend lots of money to build and equip police stations. however, people who live far from the police stations do not enjoy the feeling of safety they provide. Mobile police stations on the other hand, which are set up in big buses, can move around within their precinct which makes people feel comforted and secure. In addition, the huge amount of money, to buy the land and build large police stations, could be saved. Secondly, people will find a police check post nearby almost all the time no matter how far they live from city center. A mobile police station would be a useful resource for handling crimes since it can help adapt to criminals using more modern approaches to crime. By staying among the community, the police will have a better understanding of their citizens which may help to deter crime.

To sum up, police stations are traditionally very important buildings that are generally considered safe houses for common citizens. They are specifically designed for investigation purposes that are essential to deter crimes and maintaining law and order in society. However, some people consider them ineffective and a waste of resources. They suggest mobile police stations could meet the urgent needs of the community. Apparently, arguments from both sides carry weight and it is quite difficult to back one side. However, considering the demands of modern age, it could be a wise approach to technologically advanced police stations. In addition, a combination of technologically advanced police station buildings and new mobile police stations could help even more to make a safer society.

Main Exercises

1 Answer the questions.

Q1. How do people who live far from a police station feel?

Q2. What would police officers feel if they had no real station?

Q3. Where are mobile police stations set up in?

Q4. How can mobile police stations save government's money?

Q5. How can mobile police stations help the police to get closer to community?

2 Fill up the blanks using the words below.

replace *unimaginable* *civilization* *chaos* *trial*

1. The life without fried chickens is ……………………… .
2. Albert Einstein contributed a lot to ……………………… .
3. People would be in complete ………………………without rules.
4. Don't worry, I will temporarily ………………………you while you are on vacation.
5. You are going to be sent to prison after the ……………………… .

3 Match the phrases to those given below.

1. The police force is an important institution in every society.
2. Police stations are control centers.
3. A mobile police station would be a useful resource,
4. People who live far from the police stations.

a. It keeps the citizens safe.

b. They feel insecure.

c. For handling crimes.

d. They control the whole law and order system.

4 Summary

Fill the blanks up using the words given below and complete the summary.

traditional, staying, equipped, money, combination, institutions, security

The police force is one of the most important _____________in every society that keeps the citizens safe. However, many people think that _____________ police stations should be replaced by mobile police stations. Proponents of police stations argue that most police stations are _____________with the latest investigative equipment which is used to maintain peace. Secondly, a police station is a secure building that gives people of that community a sense of _____________. On the other hand, Opponents of police stations argue that governments spend lots of _____________to build and equip police stations while people who live far from the police stations do not enjoy the feeling of safety. Moreover, the police will have a better understanding of their citizens by _____________ among the community. In summary, it could be a wise approach to technologically advance police stations such as a _____________ of technologically advanced police station buildings and new mobile police stations.

5 Find the mistake in each sentence and correct it by reshaping the underlined words.

1. They think large police station buildings are to no importance.
2. Most police stations are equipped by the latest investigative equipment.
3. It is required of main taining peace in community.
4. People who live far to the police stations do not enjoy the feeling of safety.
5. Police will have better understand of their citizen.

6 Discussion Questions

1. Which countries have mobile police stations?
2. How big should a mobile police station be?
3. What are the potential drawbacks of mobile police stations?
4. What are the advantages of a fixd police station compared to a mobile police station?
5. Will police officers agree to work at mobile police stations? Why or why not?

7 Writing Time

What are pros and cons of mobile police stations? Are they helpful to control crimes or not? Provide reasons and examples to support your opinion.

Unit 06 Should Highways Be Toll-free?

Warm Up Exercises

01 **Answer these questions.**

1. Have you ever traveled on a highway?
2. Name at least 3 highways in South Korea.
3. When do people commonly use highways?

02 **Put the words in right column.**

House, Shopping district, Service station, Tollgate, Tollbooth, Pay

Highway	Road

Pre-Vocabulary Exercises

1 Match the words to their similar meaning.

1. Commuter	**a.** wish
2. Contribution	**b.** debated
3. Bear	**c.** endure
4. Transportation	**d.** traveler
5. Desire	**e.** traffic
6. Controversial	**f.** duty
7. Responsibility	**g.** help

2 Find the meaning of the following phrases.

1. Pay back ______________________________

2. Traffic congestion ______________________________

3. Carbon emission ______________________________

4. Domestic tourism ______________________________

Should Highways Be Toll-free?

Transportation and road infrastructure is the backbone of a country's economy. For this and other reasons commuters of every country desire high quality roads and highways. Many highways require commuters to pay tolls that the government claims will be used for the development of roads and highways. Toll taxes in many societies are a controversial issue. Some people believe that it is the state's responsibility to provide its citizens with excellent quality roads and highway networks. On the other hand, others think that those who use the highways should pay the tolls as their contribution for country's development. Do you think tolls should exist?

Proponents of tolls believe that it is every citizen's social and moral responsibility to pay back to their country. Firstly, paying taxes helps the country to update the national highway network. The money that is collected could be used for adding advanced features to the highway system including weather and traffic congestion updates. Secondly, imposing taxes on highways reduces the burden on taxpayers. Instead of using everyone's taxes to develop highways, those who use the roads frequently would bear the burden of the service they enjoy. Furthermore, heavy tolls on highways will discourage people to drive their cars all the time; therefore, people may turn to public transportation. This is will help enormously to cut country's carbon emissions. This provides a better environment for all to enjoy.

Opponents of tolls insist that tolls are an extra burden on citizens that may limit domestic tourism. Firstly, they say that it is the right of every citizen to use roads and highway infrastructure without limitations. Imposing tolls is an extra financial burden on the public that may affect their finances. Most people drive to work, and tolls are an added stress to that process. Secondly, tolls hinder a country's tourism. People may feel hesitation to leave their homes during holidays in order to explore different parts of their country because of the burden of heavy tolls. Tolls also add to the pollution in a country because more and more people use local roads instead of highways. This causes extra traffic congestion on local roads that causes heavy traffic jams. Studies say that traffic jams cause more pollution than the highway traffic.

In conclusion, highways are one of the main resources of any country that facilitate the lives of many citizens year-round. Paying tolls can help to develop and bring improvements to the road infrastructure, however, it can also pose an extra financial burden to commuters. It is important that there should be a consensus between highway authorities and the public about where and how much the tolls should be. An agreement between both parties will not only increase domestic tourism but also it will help to reduce carbon emissions.

Main Exercises

1 Answer the questions.

Q1. Why do some people hesitate to travel?

Q2. How do tolls add to the pollution in a country?

Q3. Why do most people drive?

Q4. What is the advantage of using public transportation?

Q5. What can be included to develop a highway system?

2 Fill up the blanks using the words below.

commuter *desire* *transportation* *contribution* *bear*

1. I hate taking crowded …………………...…train.
2. The Internet made a significant …………………...…to education.
3. He can …………………...…a heavy burden on his shoulder.
4. I prefer using public …………………...…, especially buses.
5. I can't stop my dog's …………………...…to run.

3 Match the phrases to those given below.

1. More and more people use local roads instead of highways.
2. Many highways require commuters to pay toll tax.
3. Those who use the roads frequently,
4. Most people drive to work.

a. This causes traffic congestion on local roads.
b. Would bear the burden of the service they enjoy.
c. It is used for the development of highways.
d. Toll taxes can be an added stress to that process.

4 Summary

Fill the blanks up using the words given below and complete the summary.

pay, development, citizen, drive, authorities, advanced, hesitation

Many highways require commuters to pay toll tax that the government claims will be used for the ______________of roads and highways. However, some people argue that those who use the highways should ______________toll tax as their contribution for country's development. Proponents of tolls believe that paying taxes helps the country to add ______________features to the highway system. Secondly, imposing taxes on highways reduces the burden on taxpayers which may discourage people to ______________their cars. On the other hand, Opponents of tolls insist that it is the right of every ______________ to use road and highway infrastructure without any limitations. Moreover, tolls hamper a country's tourism from people who may feel ______________to leave because of heavy tools. In conclusion, it is important that there should be a consensus between highway ______________and the public about where and how much the tolls should be.

5 Find the mistake in each sentence and correct it by reshaping the underlined words.

1. Toll tax will use for the development of roads and highways.
2. The money could be used to adding advanced features.
3. It will help enormous to cut country's carbone missions.
4. Imposing toll taxes are an extra financial burden.
5. For this and the other reasons commuters desire high quality roads.

6 Discussion Questions

1. Should everyone pay taxes to the country? Why or why not?
2. How do traffic jams cause more pollution than the highway traffic?
3. What are the advantages of using highways compared to using local roads?
4. What are the advantages of using local roads compared to highways?
5. How can using public transportation reduce carbon emissions?

7 Writing Time

Why do countries build highways? Are they necessary for country's progress? Provide reasons and examples to support your opinion.

Unit 07 Can AI Replace Teachers?

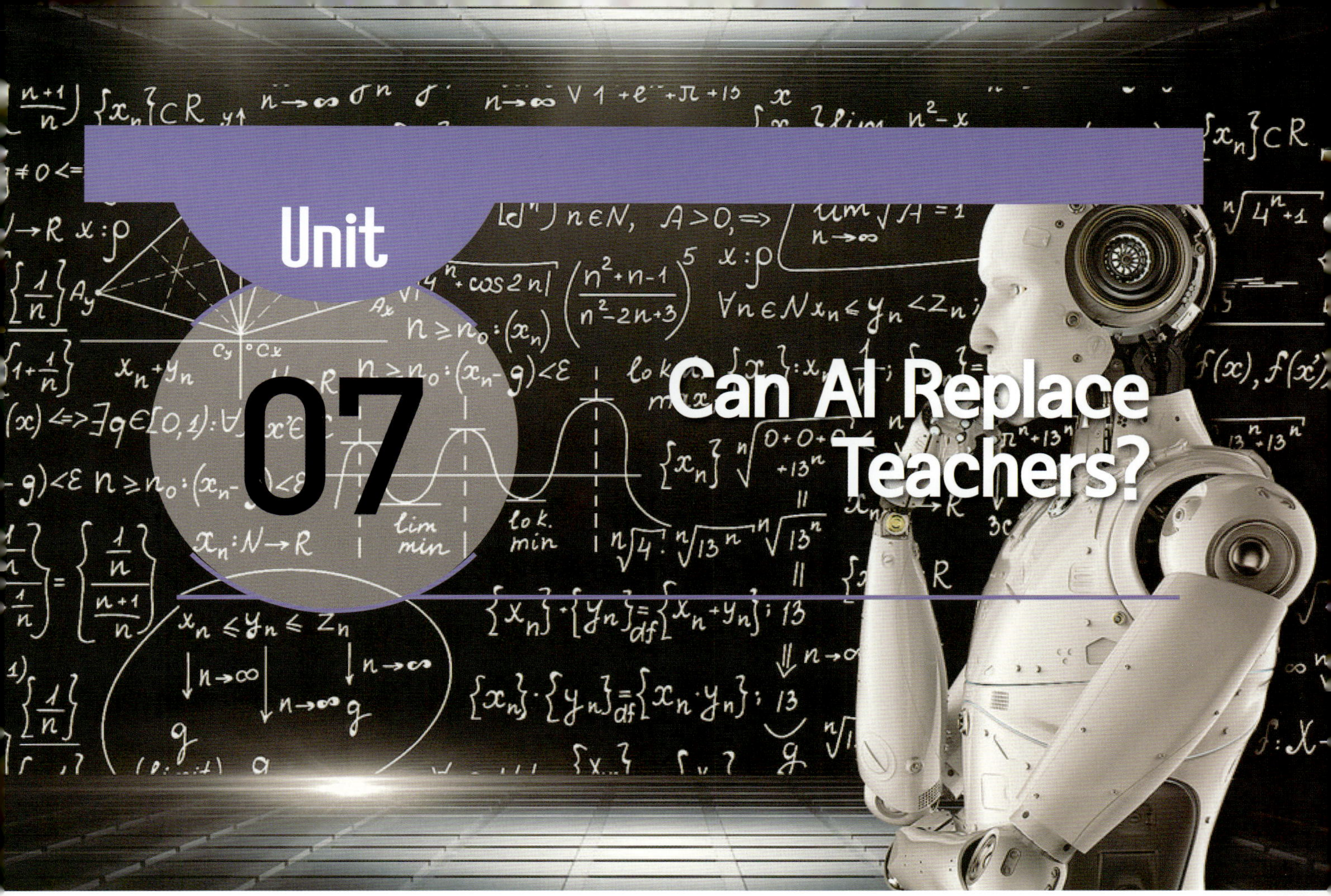

Warm Up Exercises

01 Answer these questions.

1. What is Artificial Intelligence(AI)?
2. Name any product with AI.
3. Have you ever used AI?

02 Put the words in right column.

Smarter, Life, Computer, Emotion, Durable, Technology, Blood

AI	Human

Pre-Vocabulary Exercises

1 Match the words to their similar meaning.

1. Supervision	**a.** unreal
2. Emphasize	**b.** management
3. Artificial	**c.** highlight
4. Potentially	**d.** trend
5. Expose	**e.** evaluation
6. Tide	**f.** possibly
7. Assessment	**g.** uncover

2 Find the meaning of the following phrases.

1. Central part ______________________

2. Take over ______________________

3. Financial burden ______________________

4. Placing order ______________________

Can AI Replace Teachers?

Artificial Intelligence, normally called AI, is an area of computer science that creates intelligent machines that potentially can work and react like humans. Some of the jobs that AI computers are already performing include: speech recognition, learning, planning, and problem solving. The goal of AI is to create machines that will learn and perform their jobs without any supervision. There are lots of examples of AI that is already helping humanity in many aspects of daily life including: vacuum cleaning machines, driverless cars, placing orders at cafes, etc. During past two decades, the latest computer technology has contributed to learning and helped teachers a lot to teach effectively in the classroom. Considering the dependency on technology in classrooms, many people worry that AI will ultimately take over in classrooms and teachers will have to find other jobs. Others, however, think that AI can never replace teachers and that teachers will always be required as the central part of a classroom. Do you think AI could replace teachers in the future?

People who believe that AI will replace teachers claim that the pace AI is developing at, most schools will soon be equipped by AI. Firstly, online learning and computer-based teaching is already being implemented in many educational institutions. The trend of relying on computer technologies in the classroom will only set the stage for AI to fully take over. AI is already being used in some institutions to identify students' strength, learning gaps, conduct assessments, and check their homework. Secondly, the most important reason why AI will replace teachers is the financial burden that many educational institutions bear and ultimately students have to pay for education. Having AI represents a potentially cheaper investment which will reduce the financial burden of schools to pay huge salaries to teachers every month. Furthermore, AI may be able to help resolve issues like shyness, confidence, and frustration that often arise in classroom.

Opponents of AI to replace teachers argue that although AI can teach students difficult concepts, it cannot replace a human teacher. Firstly, human teachers will always be needed to encourage students, inspire them, and manage classrooms. Education is not just teaching all the time; it is basically getting students ready to learn, feel motivated, and learn social skills that help students to find solutions to problems. Secondly, learning mainly happens through observing and imitating may be best provided by a human teacher. Knowing their teacher is not a human will affect students' ability to emphasize and imagine. Furthermore, a computer is a computer, and that can never replace a human teacher. A teacher reads a student's face, body language, appearance, and emotions in order to provide a better response. AI may never attain these abilities to deal with students' emotional states without having an understanding of students' social dynamics, circumstances at home, physical conditions, and emotional attitudes.

In conclusion, the integration of robots and AI in classrooms is changing the tide quickly. Classrooms are exposed to more and more technology-based instruction, however, considering the limitations that AI has, it may never replace teachers. In order to gain the maximum benefit for the latest technology, the best idea is to pair AI with human teachers. That will not only make teachers' jobs easier, but it will also equip students with up to date knowledge. Therefore, teachers should change their way of thinking to accepting working in cooperation with, not in competition with, AI in order to keep up with the pace of the digital era.

Main Exercises

1 Answer the questions.

Q1. Which skills can AI computers perform now?

Q2. What are the examples of AI helping humans these days?

Q3. How do some institutions use AI?

Q4. What do teachers do to provide a better response?

Q5. What is needed to deal with students' emotional states?

2 Fill up the blanks using the words below.

supervision *artificial* *expose* *potentially* *emphasize*

1. The construction is in progress safely under the .... of a manager.
2. The teacher always .... that students should study hard.
3. I need to buy some .... flowers for decorating my room.
4. We need to get rid of .... dangerous chemicals.
5. Wear sunscreen before you .... your skin to the sun.

3 Match the phrases to those given below.

1. The latest computer technology has contributed to learning.
2. Many educational institutions bear financial burden.
3. Having AI is a potentially cheaper investment.
4. A computer is computer.

a. It will reduce the financial burden of schools to pay huge salaries to teachers.

b. Ultimately students have to pay for that.

c. It helped teachers a lot to teach effectively in the classroom.

d. It can never replace a human teacher.

4 Summary

Fill the blanks up using the words given below and complete the summary.

aspects, implemented, inspire, pair, investment, imagine, ultimately

Artificial Intelligence, normally called AI, is an area of computer science and it is already helping humanity in many ____________ of daily life such as learning and helping teachers to teach effectively. However, many people worry that AI will ____________ takeover in classrooms while others think that AI can never replace teachers. People who believe that AI will replace teachers claim that online learning and computer-based teaching is already being ____________ and the trend of relying on computer technologies will only expand AI's influence in the classroom. Secondly, Having AI implies a potentially cheaper ____________ which will reduce the financial burden that ultimately students have to pay for. On the flip side, opponents of AI to replace teachers argue that human teachers will always be needed to encourage students, ____________ them, and manage classrooms. Furthermore, learning mainly happens through observing, and imitating but knowing their teacher is not a human will affect students' ability to emphasize and ____________ . To sum up, the best idea is to ____________ AI with a human teacher in order to gain the maximum benefit for the latest technology.

5 Find the mistake in each sentence and correct it by reshaping the underlined words.

1. Many people worrying that AI will take over in classroom.
2. Teachers will always be required of the central part of classroom.
3. It will also equip students by up to date knowledge.
4. Teachers will always be needed to encourage students and management classrooms.
5. Education is not just teach all the time

6 Discussion Questions

1. Is AI commercialized yet?
2. How can AI solve students' problems including shyness, confidence, and frustration?
3. When can AI be perfect to be used commercially?
4. Is AI going to dominate humans? Why or why not?
5. How do you want to use AI?

7 Writing Time

Could AI be ever able to replace human? What are pros and cons of AI? Provide reasons and examples to support your opinion.

Unit 08 Do We Need New Smartphone Every Year?

Warm Up Exercises

01 Answer these questions.

1. What is a smartphone?
2. Which smartphone do you have?
3. What is the most popular smartphone brand in the world?

02 Put the words in right column.

Internet, Phone booth, Wireless, TV, Camera, The 20th century, Thick

Smartphones	Analogue phones

Pre-Vocabulary Exercises

1 Match the words to their similar meaning.

1. Average	**a.** fall
2. Plethora	**b.** seduce
3. Tempt	**c.** disappoint
4. Hype	**d.** having know-how about something
5. Dissatisfy	**e.** common
6. Savvy	**f.** excess
7. Plummet	**g.** advertise

2 Find the meaning of the following phrases.

1. Big ticket ______________________

2. State-of-the-art ______________________

3. Dispose of ______________________

4. Keep pace with ______________________

Do We Need New Smartphones Every Year?

How often does the average person buy a new house, a new car, a new washing machine, or a new TV? These are rather big-ticket purchases and as such are rather infrequently bought. These days a big-ticket item that most people spend a huge amount of time and money on is smartphones. For many people, a smartphone is the first thing they reach for in the morning and the last thing to touch before going to bed at night. The Korean smartphone culture is one of the most advanced in the world with high speed access to Wifi, the latest smartphone models, and a plethora of smartphone accessories. However, despite the cost, the fresh, new, and state-of-the-art features of new smartphones can tempt most people to dispose of the older ones and to buy new ones every year. Some people think buying a new smartphone helps them keep pace with the people in their same social circle. On the other hand, others think it is a waste of money to buy a new smartphone every year. How often do you buy a new smartphone?

Proponents of buying a new smartphone every year claim that latest smartphone models help them to maintain access to updated features. Firstly, companies try to bait these early adopters of the latest technology by hyping the newest, freshest features when they launch a new phone. The new functions for smartphone may help users to take better pictures, use faster internet, download upgraded applications, or enjoy more secure communication. Furthermore, people may feel dissatisfied with the outdated functions of their more outdated phones. These inconveniences may include slower internet speeds, booting problems, poor voice quality, or just plain lack of interest in the older phone's design or specifications. Secondly, new smartphone models can help people to fit into certain social circles as these phones are often viewed as status symbols. New smartphone models are generally a common topic of conversation among people when they meet and can be conversation starters or a basis of common ground. Having an older model gadget may sometimes lead someone to feel isolated from their more tech savvy peers.

On the flip side, opponents of buying new smartphones every year argue that it is a wasteful financial burden on users. Firstly, new smartphones cost a lot of money and as these pricier models are being released, the prior models are plummeting in value. Disposing of used phones is not only a waste of money, but it also is harmful to the environment. In addition, over-reliance on smartphones can cause an obsession that can lead to depression and addiction. Secondly, since most smartphone companies are aware of people's obsession towards new model smartphones, they exploit this weakness to promote their products. They add one or two new features and launch new smartphones into the market through targeted advertising campaigns. The vibrant ads on TV further compel people to buy new smartphones.

To sum up, buying a new smartphone may give pleasure and satisfaction to some people; however, it also causes a financial burden and may lead to obsession at the same time. Buying a new item is primarily a personal choice, but considering cost related issues before shopping is essential, too. More importantly, in order to resist tech companies' new model gadgets, people should make decisions more based on personal needs than just superficial or temporary advantages.

Main Exercises

1 Answer the questions.

Q1. Why is the Korean smartphone culture one of the most advanced in the world?

Q2. What tempts most people to buy a new smartphone every year?

Q3. How do companies try to bait early adopters of the latest smartphone?

Q4. What functions do people generally expect for a new smartphone?

Q5. What are general problems of outdated phones?

2 Fill up the blanks using the words below.

tempt *average* *hype* *plethora* *savvy*

1. What is the ……………………score of the English test?
2. The Internet provides a ……………………of information.
3. He will try to ……………………her because she is gorgeous.
4. Ask him about your computer problems, he is computer …………………… .
5. There are too much ……………………of the new products on TV.

3 Match the phrases to those given below.

1. A smartphone is the first thing they reach for in the morning.
2. New smartphone models can help people to fit into certain social circles.
3. Over-reliance on smartphones can cause an obsession.
4. They launch new smartphones into the market through targeted advertising campaigns.

a. The vibrant ads on TV further compel people to buy new smartphone.

b. It can also lead people to depression and addiction.

c. They are generally a common topic of conversations.

d. It is also the last thing to touch before going to bed.

4 Summary

Fill the blanks up using the words given below and complete the summary.

functions, social, pace, dispose, financial, exploit, needs, up

Most people ______________ their older smartphones to buy a new one every year. Some people think buying a new smartphone helps them keep ______________ with the people in their same social circle while others think that it is a waste of money to buy new smartphone every year. Proponents of buying a new smartphone every year claim that the new ______________ for smartphone may help users to enjoy newest technology. Moreover, new smartphone models can help people to fit into certain ______________ circles as these phones are often viewed as status symbols. On the other hand, opponents of buying new smartphones every year argue that buying new smartphones is a considerable ______________ burden. Secondly, the companies ______________ people's obsession towards new smartphones to promote their products. In conclusion, people should make decisions more based on personal ______________ than just superficial or temporary advantages.

5 Find the mistake in each sentence and correct it by reshaping the underlined words.

1. How often is the average person buy a new smartphone?
2. The phones are often viewed by status symbols.
3. People may feel dissatisfied to the outdated functions.
4. New smartphones costly a lot of money.
5. The vibrant ads on TV further compel people with buy new smartphone.

6 Discussion Questions

1. How many smartphones does your family have?
2. What functions does a smartphone offer?
3. Why do companies launch a new model smartphone every now and then?
4. How long can an average smartphone work?
5. What are the main reasons people change their smartphones quite often?

7 Writing Time

Is smartphone a disaster or a blessing? What are pros and cons of smartphone? Provide reasons and examples to support your opinion.

Unit 09 Is Nomophobia Good or Bad?

Warm Up Exercises

01 Answer these questions.

1. What does it mean by nomophobia?
2. How many hours do you use your phone per day?
3. Does any of your friends have nomophobia?

02 Put the words in right column.

Horse, Car, Plane, Letter, Videotape, Book, TV, Slave, Smartphone

Past	Present

Pre-Vocabulary Exercises

1 Match the words to their similar meaning.

1. Primary	a. only
2. Merely	b. desire
3. Association	c. bond
4. Yearning	d. broad
5. Capacity	e. backbone
6. Extensive	f. Principal
7. Spine	g. ability

2 Find the meaning of the following phrases.

1. Separation anxiety ______________________
2. Abundant benefits ______________________
3. Be entangled with ______________________
4. Lead to ______________________

Is Nomophobia Good or Bad?

How do you feel when your teacher asks you not to use smartphone in class? If you are feeling a sense of separation anxiety you may have Nomophobia. Nomophobia is a term used to express the anxiety people feel when they are separated from their smartphones. It is believed that the primary cause of this anxiety is that people may worry that they are missing a call or a message. However, experts think that the main reason is users merely have a strong association with their smartphone. This strong association with their smartphone helps them feel connected with family and friends around the world. On the other hand, people's strong yearning for their smartphones may cause harm to them socially and / or physically. Some people believe that keeping your smartphone with you all the time has lots of benefits; whereas, others think that smartphones separate people from the real world and can lead to addiction.

Proponents of the widespread use of smartphones claim that they are one of the most dynamic inventions in history and that they potentially offer nearly unlimited benefits. Firstly, smartphone can be an integral part of most people's lives that give them a sense of identity. They can help people stay connected with the world through different websites and social media networks. In this age of science and technology, people are so busy that it is difficult to meet all the people we are personally related to. Hence, smartphones provide the great capacity to be in contact with loved ones at any time. Moreover, they are very convenient for getting things done as compared to using personal computers. Secondly, smartphones provide a lot of business opportunities to people who deal with their buyers and customers online. This feature of smartphones makes them an essential part of our lives. While using a computer requires people to be in their office or at home, smartphones provide mobile access to business and other useful resources which differentiates them as one of the most valuable modern items.

On the flip side, opponents of the extensive use of smartphones argue that they can be harmful for people's mental and physical health. Firstly, all electronic devices discharge radiation that can create negative effects on the human brain. Using smartphone for a major part of the day could allow the radiation to get into the bloodstream that causes different kinds of cancers. In addition, using smartphones for a long time may affect people's eyesight, causing turtleneck syndrome, and deprives people the chance to do physical activities to stay healthy. Turtleneck syndrome is also called forward head posture syndrome, when the spine goes into an anterior position. Secondly, the extensive use of smartphones can cause fear and anxiety about not having the phone which could lead to addiction. Users of smartphones may avoid making human contacts and confine themselves within their own space. Furthermore, they rely on the virtual world more and avoid making friends or meeting them in the real world.

In conclusion, the smartphone has brought abundant benefits and comforts to human life, however, their extensive use may pose risks for their users. People's greater and greater reliance on smartphones has already started damaging social relationships in many societies. Furthermore, experts predict that fear of being away from one's smartphones will only grow in the future. Smartphones are great tools to be used to get basic things done, but over-reliance on smartphones and becoming entangled with their endless features may be a dangerous path to follow. Therefore, we should think carefully about the use of smartphones before our addiction grows.

Main Exercises

1 Answer the questions.

Q1. What is the main reason of Nomophobia?

Q2. How can websites and social media networks help people?

Q3. How can electronic devices harm the human brain?

Q4. How can smartphones be harmful for people's health?

Q5. Why do people use smartphones more than PCs?

2 Fill up the blanks using the words below.

capacity *extensive* *spine* *association* *merely*

1. We are ……………………wasting our time.
2. There is a strong ……………………between Korea and Japan.
3. This job is beyond my …………………… .
4. He needs …………………… reading to complete his project.
5. A bone in my ……………………was broken.

3 Match the phrases to those given below.

1. People are so busy to meet others in person.
2. The extensive use of smartphones can…
3. Users of smartphone avoid making human contacts.
4. If you feel a sense of separation anxiety without your phone.

a. Lead to addiction.

b. You may have Nomophobia.

c. They rely on the virtual world more

d. Smartphones help them to be in contact with loved ones at any time.

4 Summary

Fill the blanks up using the words given below and complete the summary.
users, benefits, grows, harm, from, addiction

Nomophobia is a term used to express the anxiety people feel when they are separated ________________their smartphones. Some people believe that keeping your smartphone with you all the time has lots of ________________ while others think that smartphones separate people from the real world and can lead to addiction. Proponents of the widespread use of smartphones claim that they give ________________a sense of identity through websites and SNS. Moreover, smartphones provide a lot of business opportunities that computers can't. On the other hand, opponents of the extensive use of smartphones claim that they can ________________human brain, eyesight, and spine. Secondly, the extensive use of smartphones can cause fear and anxiety which end up leading to ________________. In conclusion, we should think carefully about the use of smartphone before our addiction ________________.

5 Find the mistake in each sentence and correct it by reshaping the underlined words.

1. Your teacher asks not you to use smartphone in class.
2. People may worry that they are missed a call or a message.
3. People are so busy to it is difficult to meet all the people.
4. They are very convenient for get things done.
5. It deprive people from doing physical activities.

6 Discussion Questions

1. Do you have Nomophobia? Why or why not?
2. What is the remedy for Nomophobia?
3. Is there any other new phobia?
4. What kind of phobia do you have?
5. Is there any advantage of Nomophobia?

7 Writing Time

What kind of phobia could be appeared in the future? Provide reasons and examples to support your opinion.

Unit 10

Should Children Participate in Volunteer Activities?

Warm Up Exercises

01 **Answer these questions.**

1. What does it mean by volunteering?
2. Have you ever done volunteering?
3. Have you ever donated money?

02 **Put the words in right column.**

Salary, Community, Public, Office, Promote, Spontaneous, Boss, Donate

Volunteering	Paid work

Pre-Vocabulary Exercises

1 Match the words to their similar meaning.

1. cognitive	a. imperfect
2. assign	b. appoint
3. empathy	c. productive
4. immature	d. sympathy
5. goal	e. Feeling discouraged
6. demotivation	f. aim
7. constructive	g. mental

2 Find the meaning of the following phrases.

1. Global movement ______________________
2. Link up ______________________
3. Mental capabilities ______________________
4. Take over ______________________

Should Children Participate in Volunteer Activities?

Volunteering for different activities in society has become a global movement. These days many organizations help people link up with volunteering activities all over the world. On a local level, the participation of children in volunteering is strongly encouraged by many people. They believe that encouraging children to participate in volunteer activities helps them to grow both mentally and socially. However, others think that insisting children participate in volunteer activities can cause unforeseen harm. Do you like to participate in volunteer activities?

Those who support children participating in volunteer activities claim that children can develop mentally and socially through these activities. Volunteer activities can enhance children's mental capabilities when volunteering children are given chances to take over projects which may pose a challenge to their cognitive capabilities. Most projects require problem solving skills that help develop children's thinking abilities. In addition, children may learn to understand the importance and realities of life when performing the tasks assigned to them. This may offer them a sense of responsibility which is important for the strength and maturity of young brains. Secondly, volunteer activities enhance children's social capabilities. During the tasks, they likely meet many other children with different backgrounds working for the same cause which may improve their social skills. For example, if they are working in their own community, this could be a great chance to strengthen bonds with other members of that community. It also could teach them morals and empathy toward others.

On the other hand, opponents of children's participation in volunteer activities consider it a waste of children's precious time. Firstly, in most cases, children's immature judgements and lack of experience result in a waste of both their and the organization's time which they could be spending doing more important things. While working on a task assigned to them while volunteering, children often spend most of their time playing around and may even cause disruptions for others too. This only increases the organizers' burden to not only perform their own tasks, but also to keep an eye on any children who cause problems. In some cases, children volunteer for social services in order to avoid their studies. This takes them even further from their educational goals. Secondly, some volunteer activities require basic training and better judgment. Any negligence during the task could even result in physical injury. In addition, children, who participate in volunteer activities, often use these activities as an excuse for not doing their homework. This could cause poor academic performance, and further, demotivation for their studies.

To sum up, volunteer activities are one of the most useful sources of mental and social development for children. They help children to think broadly and view the world around them more closely. However, these activities may cause some damage if not organized carefully. In order to minimize the risks and maximize children's constructive participation in volunteer activities, it is important for both the community leaders and the volunteer activity organizers to consider factors that could affect children's educational goals or school life. It may help if the activities are designed through mutual cooperation between teachers and community leaders.

Main Exercises

1 Answer the questions.

Q1. How can volunteer activities enhance children's mental capabilities?

Q2. How do volunteer activities waste children's time?

Q3. What can children learn from volunteer activities?

Q4. What can negligence during the task cause?

Q5. How can working with other children help them?

2 Fill up the blanks using the words below.

assign *goal* *cognitive* *empathy* *immature*

1. The play improves children's ....abilities.
2. The boss ....a name to newly created group.
3. I feel ....for her, she is right.
4. She is young, and still ....
5. I work hard to achieve my ....

3 Match the phrases to those given below.

1. Most projects require problem solving skills.
2. Children understand the importance of life.
3. They develop a sense of responsibility.
4. They meet other children with different backgrounds.

a. It is important for the maturity of young brains.

b. It may improve their social skills.

c. It develop children's thinking abilities.

d. While performing the tasks assigned to them.

4 Summary

Fill the blanks up using the words given below and complete the summary.
injury, judgements, over, members, unforeseen, local, immature

On a ______________ level, the participation of children in volunteering is strongly encouraged by many people. They believe that encouraging children to participate in volunteer activities helps them to grow both mentally and socially but others think that insisting children to participate in volunteer activities can cause ______________ harm. Those who support children participating in volunteer activities claim that volunteer activities can enhance children's mental capabilities while using cognitive skills to take ______________ projects. Secondly, volunteer activities enhance children's social capabilities during working with other ______________ . On the other hand, opponents of children's participation in volunteer activities insist that their ______________ judgements and lack of experience result in a waste of time since they don't participate properly. Moreover, their negligence during the task could even result in physical ______________. In conclusion, it is important for both the community leaders and the volunteer activity organizers to consider factors that could affect children's educational goals or school life.

5 Find the mistake in each sentence and correct it by reshaping the underlined words.

1. Volunteering is strong encouraged by many people.
2. Volunteering children are giving chances to take over projects.
3. Most projects require problem solved skills.
4. They like meet many other children with different backgrounds.
5. If they working in their own community, this could be a great chance to strengthen bonds.

6 Discussion Questions

1. Where can you do volunteering service?
2. Why is volunteering service not paid?
3. Which organizations do volunteering service?
4. Why do societies need volunteering service?
5. What is the problem of volunteering service?

7 Writing Time

Who needs volunteering service the most? How can we help our community? Provide reasons and examples to support your opinion.

Unit 11

Is Wearing Makeup at School Acceptable?

Warm Up Exercises

01 Answer these questions.

1. What is makeup?
2. Who mostly wears makeup?
3. Name at least 3 makeup tools.

02 Put the words in right column.

Home, Office, School, Bed, Cosmetics, Hospital

Makeup	No-makeup

Pre-Vocabulary Exercises

1 Match the words to their similar meaning.

1. Occasion	**a.** beautiful
2. Gorgeous	**b.** distrust
3. Atmosphere	**c.** fatigue
4. Weariness	**d.** circumstance
5. Hygiene	**e.** all
6. Doubt	**f.** sanitation
7. Whole	**g.** mood

2 Find the meaning of the following phrases.

1. Regardless of ________________________

2. School policy ________________________

3. In general ________________________

4. Cover up ________________________

Is Wearing Makeup at School Acceptable?

Wearing makeup is a quite common practice among teenagers around the world. Most of them start their day by wearing makeup on their faces before going to school. Even those who do not wear makeup at school on a daily basis cannot avoid it on some special occasions. Makeup can make students feel good when other people around them praise their beautiful skin, attractive eyes, or gorgeous lips. This trend of wearing makeup in school is on the rise, especially among teenage girls. Regardless of school policies about wearing makeup, most teenagers engage in at least some degree of cosmetic use. They think of it as a matter of personal choice and consider it helpful to their school life, whereas, others consider it a distraction from their studies that can harm the atmosphere of schools in general. Is wearing makeup in school really a harmful practice for teenagers?

Proponents of wearing makeup in school consider it beneficial for teenagers' personal hygiene and social relationships. Firstly, wearing makeup shows a sense of personal hygiene among teenagers which can create a positive atmosphere. People around them may appreciate them and think how careful young people are about their physical wellbeing. It also keeps teenagers fresh and active during school. For example, after studying late at night, wearing makeup wipes off teenagers' signs of weariness and helps them feel refreshed which in turn may help them to concentrate on studying for the whole day. Secondly, wearing makeup enhances teenagers' confidence and strength. Makeup covers up tiny skin imperfections that most people have. Some colorful cosmetics improve teenagers' moods, especially when they feel a little down. Wearing makeup is considered an important part of developing social relationships in school as well. In addition, some cosmetic products help to protect the skin from the sun and dust in the air.

Opponents of wearing makeup at school claim that it can be harmful for teenagers' mental health and that it negatively effects students' academics. Firstly, wearing makeup may detract from students' mental development. A strong reliance on makeup from an early age sends the message that they can only survive when wearing makeup. It could seriously alter their understanding of their personal reality and the truth about themselves which may affect their mental health. Secondly, wearing makeup in school may affect the educational atmosphere. Teenagers who focus more on their looks than studies could shift their focus from their future goals. Makeup can also create a divide between those who wear makeup in school and those who do not. Those who do not wear makeup may feel left out or uncomfortable. In addition, most cosmetics include chemicals that can sometimes cause problems for teenagers' skin e.g. irritation, swelling, or even skin infections. Furthermore, if teenagers do not wear makeup they can get more sleep in the morning instead of spending time for putting it on their faces.

In conclusion, both sides have strong arguments regarding teenagers' wearing makeup at school. There is no doubt, wearing makeup is viewed as a necessity for women of all ages these days. Makeup may represent lots of social and personal benefits, especially because teenage girls develop their awareness toward society when they use makeup and can feel more confident and powerful as members of society. However, considering the side effects of wearing makeup at school, it can damage the educational environment in school that affects students' future goals. In order to find a better solution that addresses the concerns of both sides, it is important that both teachers and students reach a mutual understanding and respect for each other's opinions. Teachers may allow some basic makeup in school so that teenagers could enjoy their freedom, and students should also respect the rules and requirements to build an excellent educational environment in school.

Main Exercises

1 Answer the questions.

Q1. How can wearing makeup affect students' mental health?

Q2. What can the chemicals in most cosmetics cause?

Q3. When can teenage girls develop their awareness toward society?

Q4. How can wearing makeup improve a sense of personal hygiene?

Q5. How can wearing makeup make students feel refreshed?

2 Fill up the blanks using the words below.

weariness *hygiene* *gorgeous* *occasion* *atmosphere*

1. The wedding is a special ………………..…… .
2. The actress looks so ………………..…in that dress.
3. I felt a tense ………………..…at the battlefield.
4. My ………………..…is due to hard work.
5. Wash your hands and be careful about your ………………..…… .

3 Match the phrases to those given below.

1. Wearing makeup wipes off teenagers'
2. Most teenagers engage in at least some degree of cosmetics.
3. Makeup can also create a divide.
4. If teenagers do not wear makeup

a. They think it as a matter of personal choice.
b. They can get more sleep in the morning.
c. Signs of weariness.
d. Those who do not wear makeup feel left out.

4 Summary

Fill the blanks up using the words given below and complete the summary.

mutual, atmosphere, school, looks, imperfections, hygiene, rely

Most students starts their day by wearing makeup on their faces before going to ______________ . However, some people consider it a distraction from their studies that can harm the ______________ of schools. Proponents of wearing makeup in school argue that wearing makeup shows a sense of personal ______________ by being careful about their physical wellbeing. Secondly, wearing makeup covers up skin's ______________ so it may enhance teenagers' confidence and strength. On the other hand, opponents of wearing makeup at school claim that wearing makeup may detract students' mental development if they ______________ too much on makeup. Furthermore, wearing makeup in school may harm the educational atmosphere when they focus more on their ______________. In conclusion, it is important that both teachers and students have mutual understanding and respect for each other's opinions.

5 Find the mistake in each sentence and correct it by reshaping the underlined words.

1. Wearing makeup shows a sense <u>for</u> personal hygiene.
2. People around <u>they</u> appreciate them.
3. People appreciate how <u>care</u> young people are about their physical wellbeing.
4. Teenagers who focus <u>much</u> on their looks than studies could shift their focus.
5. Wearing makeup is viewed <u>by</u> a necessity for women.

6 Discussion Questions

1. What do you think about men wearing makeup?
2. What else should student avoid doing in school?
3. Does wearing makeup also affect office atmosphere?
4. Can teenage students dye their hair? Why or why not?
5. Is wearing makeup really related to personal hygiene? Why or why not?

7 Writing Time

What are pros and cons of wearing makeup? Does it help students focus on their studies or it distracts them? Provide reasons and examples to support your opinion.

Unit 12 Should Military Service Be Optional for Korean Men?

Warm Up Exercises

01 Answer these questions.

1. What does it mean by military service?
2. What is the main job of military?
3. Name at least 3 types of armed forces.

02 Put the words in right column.

Gun, Tank, Patron, A/S, Training camp, Product, PR

Military	Customer Service

Pre-Vocabulary Exercises

1 Match the words to their similar meaning.

1. Tactic	**a.** workforce
2. Unavoidable	**b.** success
3. Manpower	**c.** equality
4. Prosperity	**d.** inevitable
5. Patriotism	**e.** hindrance
6. Deterrent	**f.** loyalty
7. Egalitarianism	**g.** strategy

2 Find the meaning of the following phrases.

1. Human right ______________________________

2. Violent behavior ______________________________

3. Protecting sovereignty ______________________________

4. State of war ______________________________

Should Military Service Be Optional for Korean Men?

Mandatory military service is a tactic that some countries use to ensure their military is prepared for war or any other state emergency. South Korea is one of the few countries that currently has mandatory military service regulations for all men. Most South Koreans think a stronger military is unavoidable for their country because of the threat posed by North Korea. Considering the fact that South Korea and North Korea are still in state of war, a stronger military remains one simple solution for many people in South Korea. However, some people think it is a waste of national resources and manpower. How important is mandatory military service in your opinion?

Proponents of mandatory military service consider it the backbone of country's existence and prosperity. Firstly, mandatory military service is considered a great way to promote unity among citizens. This develops a high level of patriotism that plays an important role in a country's existence. In addition, a stronger military lays the foundation for prosperity and development. A strong military deterrent has also helped contribute to Korea's development. Hence, businesses have grown and people have easier access to jobs and financial resources due to the country's stability. A country with a weaker military may struggle to improve its infrastructure and to provide safety to its citizens. Secondly, military service teaches young people lots of useful skills that they can bring into their daily lives including teamwork, responsibility, initiative, stress management, and global awareness. Furthermore, mandatory military service promotes equality among citizens. Everyone including singers, actors, doctors, and people from all walks of life have to perform the mandatory military service which is a show of egalitarianism.

Opponents of mandatory military service claim that it violates people's basic human rights and distracts young adults from their future responsibilities. Firstly, every citizen retains the right to choose the path of his/her life. A compulsory military term ignores their will to choose what they want to do. In addition, some young adults adopt violent behavior during military service that affects them and their surroundings. In some cases, violent events happen during the military service that could be fatal. Secondly, mandatory military service deters young adults' educational careers. Generally, men join military service when they are 19 or 20 years old which is one of the most crucial times in people's lives to work diligently toward their future plans. Serving in the military for almost two years distracts them from their studies and careers. Furthermore, in this age of missiles and other drone technologies, warfare may not need as many people to go to the border with guns to fight.

In conclusion, there are lots of benefits of implementing military service as a mandatory job for all men. It helps to unite the people, offers equality in society, and protects the sovereignty of the country. However, it could have some negative effects when more and more people are lead down violent paths. Another concern regarding young adults' lack of focus on education raises questions on the validity of mandatory military service. It is important that the government should find a better solution that is acceptable for the people having different opinions about this issue.

Main Exercises

1 Answer the questions.

Q1. Why do Most South Koreans think a stronger military is helpful?

Q2. What kind of skills can you learn from military service?

Q3. What lays the foundation for prosperity and development?

Q4. What are the drawbacks of a weaker military?

Q5. How can mandatory military service promote equality among citizens?

2 Fill up the blanks using the words below.

tactic *manpower* *patriotism* *unavoidable* *prosperity*

1. The army needs new ……………………… .
2. Military service is ………………………for Korean men.
3. Building a bridge needs a lot of ……………………… .
4. The soldier is a symbol of ……………………… .
5. Our future is full of ………………………, happiness, and peace.

3 Match the phrases to those given below.

1. Everyone including singer, actors, and doctors.
2. Unity develops a high level of patriotism.
3. It could have some negative effects.
4. it violates people's basic human rights.

a. Have to perform the mandatory military service in Korea.

b. When more and more people choose violent paths.

c. A compulsory military service ignores their right to choose what they want.

d. It plays an important role in a country's existence.

4 Summary

Fill the blanks up using the words given below and complete the summary.
citizens, acceptable, educational, right, resources, threat

Most South Koreans think a stronger military is unavoidable for their country because of the ________________ posed by North Korea. However, some people think it is a waste of national ________________ and manpower. Proponents of mandatory military service argue it can promote unity among citizens. Secondly, military service teaches young people lots of useful skills and promotes equality among ________________ . Opponents of mandatory military service claim that a compulsory military term ignores people's ________________ to choose what they want to do. Moreover, mandatory military service deters young adults' ________________ careers. To sum up, it is important that the government should find a better solution that is ________________ for the people having different opinions about this issue.

5 Find the mistake in each sentence and correct it by reshaping the underlined words.

1. Their military is prepared of war.
2. This develop a high level of patriotism.
3. A stronger military lies the foundation for prosperity.
4. People are lead up violent paths.
5. Military service teaches to young people lots of useful skills.

6 Discussion Questions

1. Name the countries that have mandatory military service regulations?
2. Is there any other option besides mandatory military service for Korea?
3. Why do only men have to perform mandatory military service?
4. Is it possible to reduce the term of mandatory military service?
5. When can two Koreas be united?

7 Writing Time

What could be an alternative of mandatory military service? Provide reasons and examples to support your opinion.

Unit 13 Is SNS a Better Source of News?

Warm Up Exercises

01 Answer these questions.

1. What does it mean by SNS?
2. What kind of SNS do you use?
3. Name at least 3 SNS applications that are popular these days.

02 Put the words in right column.

Tangible, Online, Offline, Telecast, Phone, Printed

SNS	Newspaper

Pre-Vocabulary Exercises

1 Match the words to their similar meaning.

1. Convey	**a.** esteemed
2. Prestigious	**b.** delay
3. Instantly	**c.** immediately
4. Viral	**d.** piece
5. Procrastination	**e.** deliver
6. Fraction	**f.** the public
7. Populace	**g.** contagious

2 Find the meaning of the following phrases.

1. Second perspective ____________________

2. In place to ____________________

3. Timely manner ____________________

4. High bar ____________________

Is SNS a Better Source of News?

A large majority of the world's population use social networking sites such as Facebook, Instagram, and Twitter. Social media sites offer their users facilities to get up to date with new information, interact with other people, convey their opinions, share photos, and engage in lots of business related activities. Many people consider obtaining news as one of the biggest benefits of social media. In this age of rapid development, people are too busy to read newspapers or watch TV to get themselves informed about the world around them. However, some consider social media as an unreliable source of information that should never replace recognized TV channels or prestigious newspapers. Do you rely more on Social Media or on TV and newspapers for news?

Proponents of social media claim that it is the fastest source of information with a huge audience. First, in the case of a disaster, social media helps information to spread instantly. In most cases, any breaking news gets viral in a short time and necessary actions can be conveyed to the affected populace in a timely manner through SNS. In addition, SNSs are a source of instant feedback. If there are any limitations or missing information regarding news or an event, users immediately offer their feedback which presents a second perspective of the incident. This is not very common on regular TV channels or newspapers where the telecasted or printed information is seldom updated based on feedback. Secondly, a vast audience provides social media legitimacy as the information is verified and commented upon by many users. Furthermore, social media has offered the audience a new and animated mode of getting information which is a step ahead of the old-fashioned and traditional media.

Opponents of using social media to obtain news rather than TV channels or newspapers argue that social media is one of the most unreliable sources that can cause distractions and procrastination. Firstly, most news available on social media is produced by immature or unprofessional people which is primarily based on their perspective rather than the facts. A TV news report is mostly produced by a team of professional journalists and that report goes through many phases of scrutiny. The high-quality controls in place to help this medium to be authentic keep the bar high for TV or newspapers. Secondly, watching TV or reading the news is a part of daily life that takes a small fraction of the time required by traditional news outlets. However, people who rely on social media as a source of news often get addicted to social media and can feel uneasy when away from it. Furthermore, a large amount of news on social media may overwhelm users and can easily distract them. On the other hand, TV or newspapers have certain sections allowing their viewers to carefully select what information they want to consume.

In conclusion, both opponents and proponents have equally important arguments in support of their choices. The use of social media for different purposes is one of the hot issues of the day. Besides lots of the benefits that SNSs represent, they could cause a major disruption in a common users' lives. With the wide growth and availability of social media, its harmful effects are already causing many social and moral problems. In order to reduce its side effects, both government and social media companies should make certain rules that confine common users within certain limits which do not harm the society. A precaution campaign should be launched to notify people about the use of social media and the ways to avoid its damages.

Main Exercises

1 Answer the questions.

Q1. Which facilities do social media sites offer to the users?

Q2. Why don't people read newspapers or watch TV these days?

Q3. Why is it a problem that the news is produced by unprofessional people?

Q4. What happens to people who rely on social media news?

Q5. Why is TV news reports credible?

2 Fill up the blanks using the words below.

instantly *prestigious* *procrastination* *viral* *convey*

1. Please ……………………this message to him.
2. He is studying hard to go to the most ……………………university.
3. I ……………………fell in love with her in our first meeting.
4. The event went ……………………within hours on SNS.
5. Your …………………… ruined our plan.

3 Match the phrases to those given below.

1. Social media has offered the audience a new mode of getting information.
2. People who rely on social media as a source of news too much.
3. TV or newspapers have certain sections.
4. Social media helps information to spread instantly.

a. Often get addicted to social media.
b. Necessary actions can be conveyed to the affected population instantly by SNS.
c. It is a step ahead of the old-fashioned media.
d. Viewers can select what information they want to consume.

4 Summary

Fill the blanks up using the words given below and complete the summary.

actions, prestigious, unprofessional, campaign, vast, unreliable, fraction

Many people consider obtaining news as one of the biggest benefits of social media. However, some consider social media as an ______________ source of information that should never replace recognized TV channels or ______________ newspapers. Proponents of social media claim that social media helps information to spread instantly so that necessary ______________ can be taken in time. Secondly, a ______________ audience provides social media legitimacy as the information is verified and commented upon by many users. Opponents of using social media to obtain news believe most news available on social media is produced by immature or ______________ people and it can cause distractions. Moreover, watching TV or reading the news is a part of daily life that takes a short ______________ of the time but some people indulge in social media. In conclusion, a precaution ______________ should be launched to notify people about the use of social media and the ways to avoid its damages.

5 Find the mistake in each sentence and correct it by reshaping the underlined words.

1. SNS enables their users to be interacted with other people.
2. Social media helps information to spread instant.
3. Printed information is seldom updating based on feedback.
4. Its harmful affects are already causing many social and moral problems.
5. Most news available on social media is producing by immature or unprofessional people.

6 Discussion Questions

1. What are advantages of TV?
2. What are advantages of Newspaper?
3. What are advantages of SNS?
4. Which news topics are you interested in?
5. What is your favorite SNS?

7 Writing Time

Do you prefer SNS or newspaper? Provide reasons and examples to support your opinion.

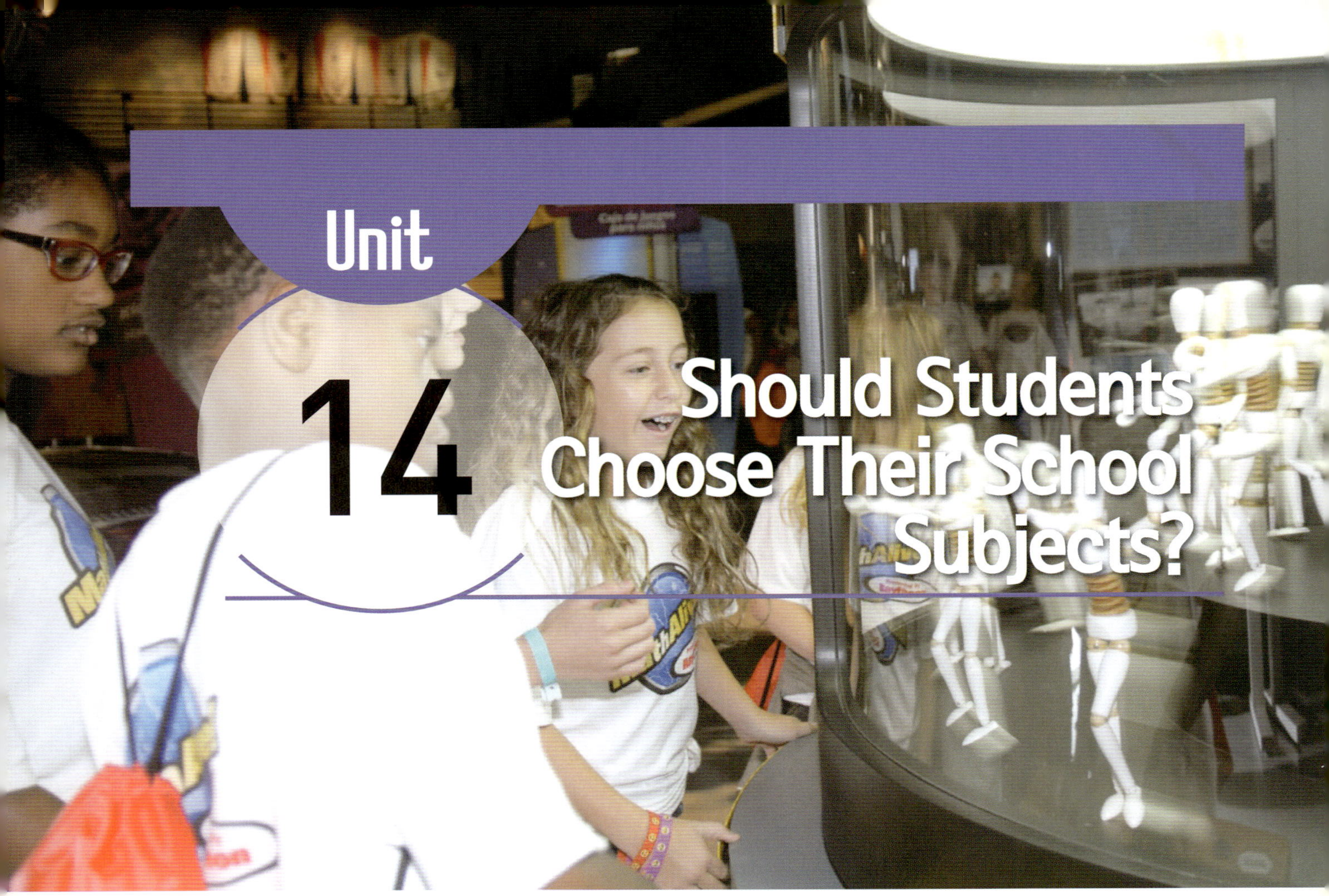

Unit 14 Should Students Choose Their School Subjects?

Warm Up Exercises

01 **Answer these questions.**

1. What is your favorite school subject?
2. Name at least 5 school subjects.
3. What is your least favorite school subject?

02 **Put the words in right column.**

Language, Grammar, Calculator, Words, Translation, Formula, Numbers

Math	English

Pre-Vocabulary Exercises

1 Match the words to their similar meaning.

1. Useless	**a.** worthless
2. Command	**b.** similarly
3. Enormously	**c.** administrator
4. Equally	**d.** perspctive
5. Valid	**e.** extremely
6. Coordinator	**f.** grasp
7. Aspect	**g.** effective

2 Find the meaning of the following phrases.

1. Future goal ______________________

2. Meet the need ______________________

3. Academic freedom ______________________

4. In favor of ______________________

Should Students Choose Their School Subjects?

School is one of the most important parts of our lives. School not only helps students learn necessary concepts and skills, but it also allows students to interact with other students socially, academically, and emotionally. Most schools teach subjects as part of curriculum that the curriculum coordinators believe will benefit the students in the future. Each subject that is taught in school develops student's knowledge of humanity, real life, and social relations. School subjects also help them to set their future goals. Some people think that teaching students so many different subjects in school is useless as they might not be interested in all of these subjects. They suggest that students must have the right to choose their subjects based on their interests. Do you think students should be able to choose their favorite school subjects or not?

Proponents of required school subjects believe that they help students to develop a broader understanding of the various aspects of life. Firstly, school subjects are mostly chosen to meet the needs of student's basic understanding of life. They need at least a basic command of mathematics, science, geography, social studies, etc. Without these subjects, they may feel ignorant when communicating with the people around them. Secondly, if students are given the choice to pick the subjects they want, they may just choose the subjects their friends are choosing without considering the importance of those subjects. This is because most students may be too immature to decide their own curriculum. In addition, because of their weak judgment, they may choose one subject again and again. For example, if they like geography, they may choose geography again and again. This will limit their knowledge of other important parts of human life that may affect their future.

Proponents of academic freedom in school claim that it is a students' basic right to choose their favorite subjects to study. Firstly, choosing their favorite subjects will help them to focus more and they will take greater interest in those subjects. This will help teachers enormously since they do not need to be worried about motivating students to study. Secondly, choosing their favorite subjects may help students to define their futures. Studying lots of subjects may confuse students about what they want to be in the future. When you ask a 5-year-old what they want to be, they may instantly respond doctor, engineer, singer, etc. However, a 13-year-old child may not respond to this question and will simply reply, I do not know yet. In addition, giving students a choice to pick subject they want to learn about will give them more chances to think about their future and gain a better understanding about their favorite subjects. That will help their mental development and let them become more mature.

In conclusion, both arguments in favor of and against students choosing their own school subjects are equally important. As the world is more and more technology dependent, the schools may want to reconsider the way they have been teaching students. In the modern age, TV, computers, and SNS can teach children lots of things that can help them to obtain a clear perspective about the world. Therefore, the idea may not be valid in the future as it may burden students with lots of subjects regardless of their personal choices. There must be a revival of school policy that may reduce some subjects and add subjects based on student's preferences.

Main Exercises

1 Answer the questions.

Q1. What happens if students are given the choice to pick the subjects they want?

Q2. What happens if they choose the same subjects again and again?

Q3. What can TV, computers, and SNS teach children better?

Q4. How do the subjects students learn in school help them?

Q5. How can choosing favorite subjects help students?

2 Fill up the blanks using the words below.

command *useless* *equally* *enormously* *valid*

1. This phone is ...., it is broken.
2. His good ....of English is his specialty.
3. The rich guy's watch is ....expensive.
4. All people should be treated ....
5. He gave lots of .... reasons to justify his claim.

3 Match the phrases to those given below.

1. The schools may want to reconsider their teaching styles.
2. Schools allow students to interact with other students,
3. They may only choose the subjects their friends are choosing.
4. Studying lots of subjects may confuse students about their future.

a. As the world is more and more technology dependent.

b. Their favorite subjects may help them to think about their future.

c. Because they're too immature to decide.

d. Socially, academically, and emotionally.

4 Summary

Fill the blanks up using the words given below and complete the summary.
revival, importance, meet, different, interest, coordinators

Most schools teach subjects as part of curriculum that the curriculum ______________ believe will benefit the students in the future. However, some people think that teaching students so many ______________ subjects in school is useless as they might not be interested in all of these subjects and students should be able to choose their favorite school subjects. Proponents of required school subjects believe that school subjects are mostly chosen to ______________ the needs of student's basic understanding of life. Secondly, students may just choose the subjects their friends are choosing without considering the ______________ of those subjects since they are too young to make a judgment. On the flip side, opponents of academic freedom in school claim that choosing their favorite subjects will help them to focus more and they will take greater ______________ in those subjects. Secondly, giving students a choice to pick subject will give them more chances to think about their future. In conclusion, there must be a ______________ of school policy that may reduce some subjects and add subjects based on student's preferences.

5 Find the mistake in each sentence and correct it by reshaping the underlined words.

1. Each subject that is teached in school develops student's knowledge.
2. School subjects are mostly chose to meet the needs of student's basic understanding of life.
3. They do not need to be worried about motivating students to studying.
4. There must be a revival of school policy that adds subjects base on student's preferences.
5. School is one of the most important part of ourlives.

6 Discussion Questions

1. If you have the freedom to choose subjects, which subjects are you going to pick at first?
2. What other freedom do students also need?
3. Why can university students choose their favorite subjects?
4. What subjects do you hate? why?
5. Is there any side-effect to academic freedom?

7 Writing Time

Which side are you on, academic freedom or required school subjects? And why? Provide reasons and examples to support your opinion.

Unit 15

Should We Use Fingerprints for Shopping?

Warm Up Exercises

01 **Answer these questions.**

1. What is a fingerprint?
2. When do people commonly use fingerprints?
3. How do fingerprints look like?

02 **Put the words in right column.**

Memorize, Inborn, Numbers, Biological, Adjustable, Body

Fingerprint	Password

Pre-Vocabulary Exercises

1 Match the words to their similar meaning.

1. Whorl	**a.** cheat
2. Intricate	**b.** duplicate
3. Precisely	**c.** complex
4. Replicate	**d.** a circular arrangement
5. Fraud	**e.** bother
6. Breach	**f.** break
7. Hassle	**g.** accurately

2 Find the meaning of the following phrases.

1. Biometric identification ______________________________

2. Heavy bills ______________________________

3. Modern age ______________________________

4. Security threat ______________________________

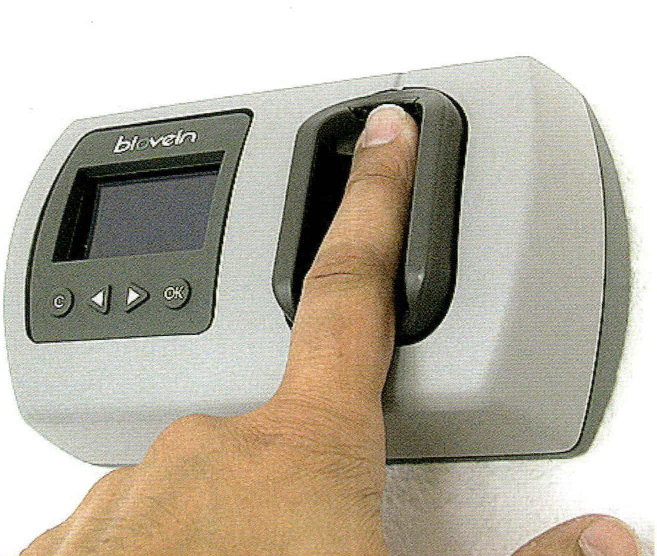

Should We Use Fingerprints for Shopping?

Fingerprints are one of the most unique structures in this universe as no two are alike. The patterns, loops, arches, and whorls in our skin form an intricate and unique design which helps to precisely identify us. It is impossible to have two people with identical fingerprints. Development of technology has enabled scientists to use fingerprints for not only identification purposes at the airports, but also for maintaining each person's biodata in a main computer system. Biometric identification is an example of technology that helps authorities easily recognize people. In recent years, fingerprints are even used for shopping in malls. Most people think it is a beneficial way to address customers' needs for shopping in the modern age, whereas others consider it a big security threat for customers. Do you think fingerprints should be used for shopping, or not?

Proponents of the use of fingerprints for shopping claim that it can help customers to enjoy shopping more conveniently. Firstly, using fingerprints to pay for purchased items is the safest way to shop. People do not need to carry credit cards or cash each time they go shopping. There are many chances to get one's credit cards or money stolen. However, your fingerprints are always with you and they cannot be replicated. In addition, lots of credit card fraud could be prevented by using fingerprints when shopping. Secondly, using fingerprints for shopping helps people to save time. People do not need to find their credit cards or count cash in their bags each time they have to pay. A simple biometric recognition scan could allow customers to pay for their shopping without any wasted time. Furthermore, customers' current amount of hassle to memorize their passwords would be reduced.

Opponents of using fingerprints for shopping argue that it can be harmful for customers in many ways. Firstly, hackers and criminals likely can find a way to replicate fingerprints in order to steal money. There are lots of examples which show how easily hackers have breached fingerprint security in order to gain access to personal data. Apple's Touch ID system was hacked just one day after its launch when hackers photographed a fingerprint left on the glass screen of the phone. Through an ordinary scanner, they created a fake fingerprint that provided them the access to the phone. Secondly, using fingerprints for shopping will encourage people to waste money. Since there is no hassle or thought as with cash or credit cards, people will just pay and forget their transactions. This may affect their budget and they may end up paying heavy bills at the end of the month.

To sum up, the discovery of fingerprint recognition as a source of payment is a great scientific breakthrough. It is a step further towards the goal of human convenience and comfort. Not only does it free people from the responsibilities of keeping credit cards or cash with them all the time in their wallets, it also saves a lot of time. As mentioned earlier, there are security threats associated with fingerprints payment methods. Criminals always look for the ways to steal personal information in order to gain personal benefit. It would be very important for the government to keep a very close eye on the security of this revolutionary discovery so that no one could abuse it. In addition, customers may choose extra security measures including one or two step verification of personal information when using fingerprints for shopping.

Main Exercises

1 Answer the questions.

Q1. Why are fingerprints one of the most unique structures?

Q2. How do fingerprints help people save time?

Q3. What is the example of hackers breaching fingerprint security?

Q4. How can fingerprints be hacked through phones?

Q5. What are the recommendations regarding using fingerprints for shopping?

2 Fill up the blanks using the words below.

precisely *fraud* *intricate* *replicated* *hassle*

1. The maze is very ....
2. Please call me at 3'o clock ....
3. The inspector found the watch fake since it is ....
4. She received a 10-year sentence for ....
5. Cleaning my room is a real ....

3 Match the phrases to those given below.

1. People do not need to carry credit cards or cash each time they go shopping.
2. Biometric identification is one of the examples.
3. There is no hassle as with cash or credit cards.
4. This may affect their budget.

a. Lots of credit card fraud could be prevented by using fingerprints when shopping.

b. People will just pay and forget their transactions.

c. They may end up paying heavy bills at the end of the month.

d. It helps authorities easily recognize people.

4 Summary

Fill the blanks up using the words given below and complete the summary.
save, safest, eye, glass, biodata, waste fingerprints

Development of technology has enabled scientists use fingerprints for maintaining each person's ______________ in a computer system so fingerprints are now even used for shopping in malls. However, some people consider it a big security threat. Proponents of the use of fingerprints for shopping argue that it is the ______________ way to shop since people do not need to carry credit cards or cash. Moreover, s simple biometric recognition scan helps people to ______________ time and get rid of hassle to memorize their passwords. On the other hand, Opponents of using ______________ for shopping insist that hackers and criminals likely can find a way to replicate fingerprints which is left on the ______________ or something. Secondly, using fingerprints for shopping is so simple that it will encourage people to ______________ money. In conclusion, it would be very important for the government to keep a very close ______________ on the security of fingerprint usage so that no one could abuse it.

5 Find the mistake in each sentence and correct it by reshaping the underlined words.

1. There are many chances to get one's credit cards or money steal.
2. Hackers and criminals like can find a way to replicate fingerprints in order to steal money.
3. They created a fake fingerprint that provided them the access for the phone.
4. They may end up paid heavy bills.
5. There are security threats associating with fingerprints payment methods.

6 Discussion Questions

1. Can fingerprints be erased or changed?
2. How are fingerprints formed?
3. When do you use your fingerprints?
4. What are the other security systems besides fingerprints and password?
5. How do fingerprints make shopping easier?

7 Writing Time

Which security system could be safer and more useful for shopping than fingerprints? Provide reasons and examples to support your opinion.

Unit 16 Should Cram Schools Operate after 10pm?

Warm Up Exercises

01 **Answer these questions.**

1. What is a cram school?
2. Have you ever attended a cram school?
3. What time do you usually go to bed at night?

02 **Put the words in right column.**

More expensive, Private, Cheaper, Uniform, Alternative, Various, Additional

Cram school	Public school

Pre-Vocabulary Exercises

1 Match the words to their similar meaning.

1. Excessive	a. rivalry
2. Competition	b. hinder
3. Hamper	c. academy
4. Needy	d. poor
5. Violation	e. desire
6. Institution	f. too much
7. Drive	g. offense

2 Find the meaning of the following phrases.

1. Pass exam ______________________
2. Regular basis ______________________
3. Mental strain ______________________
4. Extra study ______________________

Should Cram Schools Operate after 10pm?

Studying is a difficult task for most students that sometimes requires them to go to another institution for extra study after their regular schooling. Cram schools are a kind of extra school that helps students to study hard till late at night in order to meet certain goals, including passing the university entrance examinations. These are privately owned schools wherein parents pay extra money for their children's education. Korea is one of the countries where cram schools are dominating the private education industry and students may only study there till 10pm according to new law. Lots of people think imposing restriction on cram schools to operate after 10 at night helps students to relax, prepare for next day, and spend more time with families; whereas, opponents of the new law say that it restricts cram schools and consider this law to be unfair. They think this is a matter of personal choice where students should be able to study until they want. Should cram schools be allowed to operate till late night again as they used to in the past?

Proponents of the new law that restricts cram schools to work after 10 pm insist that it helps to curtail dangerously excessive competition among students to get into top universities. Firstly, students need to take some rest after a long day in order to be fresh and ready for next day. Studying till late at night on a regular basis damages students' physical and mental health. They feel tired, sleepy, stressed, and even depressed. Therefore, a ban on cram schools operating after 10pm may help students to spend more time with their family and friends and that gives them physical relief and mental peace. Secondly, if students stay in cram schools till late at night, they may not get any chance to learn to think independently. This may hinder their mental growth and creativity. Furthermore, humans learn more by experience rather than staying for long hours in classrooms.

Opponents of the new law argue that it limits students' freedom to choose their own study time and place. Firstly, students are one of the most important parts of any society. Prohibiting them from studying at cram schools after 10 pm may hamper their chances to get help from teachers and friends. In a competitive society like Korea, students are aware of the value of hard work in order to get success in the future. Closing cram schools at 10 may negatively affect their ability to compete against other students. Secondly, in most cases, teachers in schools cover the curriculum at a faster pace that is difficult for some students to follow. Therefore, they need extra help from the teachers at cram schools in order to understand what is taught in class. In addition, closing cram schools at 10pm is a waste of such a useful resource for needy students who have the energy and the drive to study hard till late at night.

In conclusion, the law mentioned above was made to reduce unnecessary competition in education that may cause too much mental strain for some students. Another purpose of implementing that law was to offer students more chances to relax and spend time with family or friends. However, some people consider this law to be a violation of the students' basic human right to make their own choices. In order to address the concerns of both sides, the government should find solutions through careful discussion and consideration with parents and students. A consensus may help to make the education system more effective in order to reduce students' anxiety regarding study till late at night.

Main Exercises

1 Answer the questions.

Q1. How does spending more time with family help students?

Q2. How does studying till late at night harm students?

Q3. Which examination do cram schools mostly prepare for?

Q4. What happens if students spend too much time in cram schools?

Q5. What makes it difficult for Korean students to achieve success?

2 Fill up the blanks using the words below.

needy *violation* *hampers* *excessive* *competition*

1. ....drinking is harmful to your health.
2. He became the winner of the ....
3. Using smartphone ....sleep at night.
4. Doctors help ....people.
5. .... of the law can put you in trouble.

3 Match the phrases to those given below.

1. Cram schools are privately owned schools.
2. It helps to curtail the dangerously excessive competition among students.
3. Studying till late at night damages students' physical and mental health.
4. The ban on cram schools may help students.

a. They feel tired, sleepy, stressed, and even depressed.

b. To spend more time with their family and friends.

c. Who want to get into top universities.

d. Parents pay extra money for their children's education.

4 Summary

Fill the blanks up using the words given below and complete the summary.

till, night, negatively, independently, rest, dominating, pace

Cram schools are a kind of extra school that helps students to study hard till late at ______________ and Korea is one of the countries where cram schools are ______________ the private education industry. According to the new law on cram schools, students may only study there ______________ 10pm but opponents of the new law say this is unfair. Proponents of the new law argue that students need to take some ______________ after a long day in order to be fresh and ready for next day. Secondly, they may not get any chance to learn to think ______________ if students stay in cram schools till late at night. On the other hand, Opponents of the new law believe it may hamper their chances to get help and ______________ affect their ability to survive in Korea's competitive society. Moreover, they need extra help from the teachers at cram schools when they can't keep ______________ with the curriculum. In conclusion, the government should find solutions through careful discussion and consideration with parents and students.

5 Find the mistake in each sentence and correct it by reshaping the underlined words.

1. These are private owned schools.
2. Should cram schools be allowed to operate till late at night again as they use to in the past?
3. Humans learn more by experience rather than stay for long hours in classrooms.
4. They feel tire, sleepy, stressed, and even depressed.
5. Students are aware with the value of hard work.

6 Discussion Questions

1. Why do parents want their children to study hard?
2. Why are cram schools prevalent in Korea?
3. Are cram schools essential for students? Why or why not?
4. What do you want to learn in a cram school?
5. Are internet lecture services helpful for students? Why or why not?

7 Writing Time

Is crams school culture affecting Korean society negatively or positively? Provide reasons and examples to support your opinion.

| 저자약력 |

About the Author

Bilal Qureshi earned his Doctorate degree in TESOL at Queen's University Belfast, UK and currently teaches at Seokyeong University Seoul. He has been interested in variety of issues related to second language learners' motivation and skill development; and this series of books shows his dedication and passion toward this goal. Email: qureshi@skuniv.ac.kr

Acknowledgement

I want to thank everyone who helped me through this process especially the reviewer and proofreader Professor David Miller, whose hard work motivated me a lot. I also show my appreciation to Professor Uk Chang from Duksung Women's University, Zeeshan Qureshi, Kim Bora, Jeong MinGyu, Hwang Junsook, and above all, my mother whose constant encouragement helped me complete this project.

Progressive Debate Active 3

2019년 1월 20일 1판 1쇄 인쇄
2019년 1월 25일 1판 1쇄 발행

저 자 | BILAL QURESHI
발행인 | 이수영
발행처 | 도서출판 청람
서울시 마포구 독막로 288(대흥동, 세양상가 109호)
전 화 | 02)3272-2601~2
팩 스 | 02)3272-2603
이메일 | crbooks@daum.net
홈페이지 | http://www.crbooks.co.kr
등 록 | 2000.8.26. 제6-0509호

ISBN 978-89-5972-669-1 93740 [정가 13,000원]

Audio files:
www.crbooks.co.kr/progressiveActive3/